Please
return
materials
on time

IE

Printed and bound in the UK by MPG Books, Bodmin

Published by Sanctuary Publishing Limited, Sanctuary House, 45-53 Sinclair Road, London W14 0NS, United Kingdom

www.sanctuarypublishing.com

Photo credits in order of appearance: 1. George Bernard/Science Photo Library 2. Prof K Seddon & Dr T Evans/Queen's University, Belfast/Science Photo Library 3-9. Getty Images Inc 10. George Bernard/Science Photo Library 11. George Bernard/Science Photo Library 12. Stanley B Burns MD & The Burns Archive New York/Science Photo Library 13-19. Getty Images Inc 20. Catherine Karnow/Corbis 21. Getty Images Inc 22. Stanley B Burns MD & The Burns Archive New York/Science Photo Library 23. Zephyr/Science Photo Library 24. Zephyr/Science Photo Library 25. St. Bartholomew's Hospital/Science Photo Library 26. Moredun Animal Health Ltd/Science Photo Library 27. Eye of Science/Science Photo Library 28. Science Photo Library 29. Biophoto Associates/Science Photo Library 30. Dr Arthur Tucker/Science Photo Library 31. Pascal Goetgheluck/Science Photo Library 32. Susumu Nishinaga/Science Photo Library 33. Tek Image/Science Photo Library 34. Getty Images Inc 35. Cliff Bevan/PYMCA

ISBN: 1-86074-419-2

This is
NICOTINE

KAREN FARRINGTON

CONTENTS

INTRODUCTION

To smoke or not to smoke - that is the question. It is possible that, as a trendy guy, Shakespeare was puffing away on a pipe even as he wrote *Hamlet*, from which the above phrase has been borrowed and butchered. If he didn't his audiences certainly did as pipes – the favourite way of taking tobacco at the time – have been uncovered at the site of the Globe, Shakespeare's London theatre.

As a pastime, smoking is notorious rather than glorious. Light up a cigarette and it leaves you sick, smelly and broke. Yet millions of people ignite 20, 40 or more paper tubes stuffed with shreds of tobacco every day of their lives, in full knowledge of its worst side effects. Countless millions have been spent on broadcasting a 'don't smoke' message loud and clear, but mystifyingly a significant proportion of the population doesn't listen. At first glance, society's preoccupation with smoking is a dangerous obsession that appears wanton and baffling. But that's just one view. A cigarette is more, much more, than just a tobacco stick and nicotine fix. A smoke speaks volumes when words cannot be trusted for the task. Oh, there's much more to smoking than meets the eye.

Smoking is inextricably linked with image. In films, on television, on the street, the view that smoking is 'cool' and sexy and a symbol of the talented was knitted into the fabric of society for years. It has been a difficult tradition to unpick.

With every purchase the smoker bought into a world of glamour and high fashion. Just about all the 20th-century icons smoked, including Winston Churchill, Al Capone, Che Guevara, John Lennon, James Bond, James Dean, Joni Mitchell, Franklin D Roosevelt, Fats Waller, David Niven,

Yul Brynner, Josef Stalin, Frank Sinatra, Bob Dylan, Damien Hirst, Betty Grable, Bette Davis, Humphrey Bogart, Nat 'King' Cole, Noël Coward, Sigmund Freud, Steve McQueen, Spencer Tracy, Kate Moss, and Sarah Jessica Parker. It's difficult to scratch together a list of social heroes who haven't been known for a nicotine habit. All these icons have been photographed with haloes of smoke hanging around their heads. In the collective subconscious, the cigarette has become linked to the great and the good. Even today the images are so seductive it is easy to believe that, with a cigarette in your hand, you will be elevated up the ranks towards that of international idol. Surely some of the style and panache associated with smoking will rub off?

According to the American Cancer Society there are more than 1.2 billion smokers worldwide.

A long, low draw on a filter tip, followed by the slow, lazy exhalation of smoke clouds conjures up a vision of someone who is calm and in control. As a crisis unfolds the non-smoker might run from room to room, arms aloft, all a-panic. A counterpart who smokes, however, sits down, lights up and bears the patient expression of someone contemplating a perfect response. This is a reflex action on the part of smokers. The icy exterior is not for real, of course, as the smoker is surely hiding just as much agitation and trepidation. But hey, appearances count.

Like them or loathe them, cigarettes – aka tabs, smokes, fags, snouts, rollies and baccy – have won a special place in society. For 500 years tobacco has played its part in world history, never a leading character but always in a supporting role. It is difficult to pinpoint just why it played such a pre-eminent part in the unfolding story of mankind. After all, today's uses of tobacco may not have been entirely obvious in the 16th century. No one seeing the virgin tobacco plant swaying in the breeze could immediately imagine it as the source of cigarettes and its associated pleasures and pains. Amazing really that after Sir Walter Raleigh brought back tobacco from the New World to Britain the smoking habit caught on at all. Who would have believed that anyone would hand over good money for a substance that they then set on fire, taking pleasure in the smoke?

The American comic Bob Newhart made memorable comedy when

he portrayed a likely telephone conversation between himself as the British importer, ignorant of tobacco and its uses, and the man he tags as 'nutty Walt'.

He roars with laughter at the suggestion of putting tobacco up the nose as snuff users do. Newhart then recounts the explanation for other uses of tobacco given by the (imaginary) Raleigh.

'You can shred it up...put it on a piece of paper...and roll it up... [laughs] Don't tell me, Walt, you stick it in your ear, right Walt?'

Newhart goes on to express frank disbelief that people would ever put leaves between their lips and set light to them, revelling in the smoke. Surely you could stand in front of a fireplace and benefit from the same effect? The make-believe telephone call ends with the words 'Don't call us, we'll call you.'

But the fad caught on and tobacco in its many forms has been ingrained in society for years. Cigarettes are galvanizing, gratifying and thoroughly dependable, a soother and a stimulant. For the smoker his best friend is never more than an arm's length away. It's anger management in a stick. Anecdotal evidence says that droves of people in New York either smoked for the first time or began the habit again following the terrorist attacks in the city on 11 September 2001. Their aim was to relieve the tension that was as palpable as the heavy smoke pall hanging across the ruins of the twin towers.

> In 1997 cigarette smoking accounted for an estimated 117,400 of the total 628,000 deaths in the United Kingdom. Cigarette smoking is thus responsible for approximately one in every five deaths in Britain. This annual mortality translates into an average of 2,300 people killed by smoking every week, 320 every day, and 13 every hour. Royal College of Physicians

However, few smokers are actively keen for their children to begin the habit and it is likely that if cigarettes were invented today they would be banned straight away.

Yet there's still more to this contentious issue. Smoking has escalated into a bitter international 'tar wars', being waged without the prospect of a peace-keeping force. One side dispatches an argument like a nuclear missile that seems to leave the other for dead. But inevitably a response comes whistling back, delivering a belting body blow. Just by way of an example, committed non-smokers claim that 90 per cent of all lung cancer cases are caused by smoking. 'Really?' say the defenders of the habit. 'So how come lung cancer was so low in Japan where smoking rates among men were traditionally high?' Both camps feel utter scorn and contempt for the antics of the opposition and each speaks with a ranting, self-righteous air. The battleground is not very pretty.

> 'A cigarette is the perfect type of a perfect pleasure. It is exquisite, and it leaves one unsatisfied. What more can one want?' *The Picture Of Dorian Gray* by Oscar Wilde (1854-1900)

The big problem with cigarettes is that they can kill you. And it's generally not a quick, clean kind of death.

Young people – and some older ones – believe they are immortal. As you puff away at 18 the cause of your death some 60 years down the line is the last thing on your mind. So it is easy to blot out the agony that may or may not strike sometime in the future in favour of the instant fulfilment that smoking a cigarette brings now. Even when smokers are presented with immediate personal health risks they are often reluctant to quit. Fear is not enough. A sizeable number of people – smokers and non-smokers – believe that measures designed to prevent people smoking are an attack on personal liberty.

And some have never been convinced that smoking is at all dangerous. Mark Twain, writing on his 70th birthday in 1905, was an advocate of this point of view. 'I have made it a rule never to smoke more than one cigar at a time. I have no other restriction as regards smoking.

'I do not know just when I began smoking. I only know that it was in my father's lifetime and that I was discreet. He passed from this life early in 1847, when I was a shade past 11, ever since then I have smoked publicly. As an example to others, and not that I care for moderation myself, it has always been my practice never to smoke when asleep and never to refrain when awake.'

Wisely, he conceded that smoking non-stop for 60 years would not be the answer for everyone aiming to achieve a 70th birthday. For the record Samuel Longhorne Clemens, as he was originally called before adopting the pseudonym of Mark Twain, lived for a further five years.

But it is only right to colour accounts of smoking and cigarettes with some of the vivid statistics knocking around today.

Here's the real deal with cigarettes, so take a deep breath. Smoking can cause lung cancer, heart disease, emphysema, bronchitis and arterial disease – and appears a root cause of other cancers, including those of the mouth and throat. And this is by no means a complete list, it's just a start.

Tobacco kills one person every ten seconds, which computes to about four million deaths per year. In the West smoking is thought to be the cause of about half of all cancer deaths and at least 90 per cent of lung cancer deaths.

All of this gruesome information is relatively fresh in the history of tobacco and smoking. It wasn't until the 1950s that the link between smoking and lung cancer went public. You'd think this galling disclosure would be sufficient to deter the generations that grew up in the '60s, '70s, and thereafter from taking so much as one suck at a cigarette. Not so. Although there was a drop in the amount of educated male smokers in the West, there has been no sustained fall in the number of smokers among women, the working classes and the Third World.

> Cigarette smoke is acidic and the nicotine from it is absorbed through the lungs. Pipe and cigar smoke is alkaline and the nicotine is absorbed through the mouth.

Boatloads of literature have been produced in the last half-century about the health problems posed by smoking yet still a vast number of people take no notice of the warnings whatsoever and continue to puff away.

Why do they do it? Well, the sad fact is many don't appear able to help themselves. True, there are a sizeable number of people who are happy smokers. They enjoy it, do it willingly and have no intention of giving up – and good luck to them. But there are lots for whom it is a drag. They long to kick the habit, stub it out and inhabit a smoke-free zone, but they can't. These are, apparently, addicts who find it hard to help themselves.

Inside every tobacco leaf there is a substance called nicotine, which is highly addictive and extremely toxic. Nicotine is so potent that it is used as an insecticide – so it is bad for bugs as well as for humans. Indeed, pound for pound, nicotine is more dangerous than both arsenic and strychnine. As long ago as 1665 diarist Samuel Pepys recorded a Royal Society experiment in which a cat died after being fed 'a drop of distilled oil of tobacco'.

Of course, the single cigarette bears quantities of nicotine that the body can tolerate. No one knows the exact science behind it but it is widely believed that every inhalation brings nicotine to the brain in a succession of rapid 'hits', creating a dependency. Smoking is a very intense habit, with every cigarette delivering about ten hits of nicotine so anyone on a packet a day would be experiencing something in the order of 200 in 24 hours. Whatever

> 'Every 30 seconds someone somewhere in the world dies of lung cancer. It is the ninth most common cause of death in the world and the most common form of cancer. Each year 1.25 million people die from it.' Roy Castle, International Centre for Lung Cancer Research

drugs you choose to take in your life, you will never come across one as addictive as nicotine. The longer people smoke, the harder it is to quit. Nicotine isn't the most harmful element of cigarettes but it is the one thing that makes people come back for more.

Nicotine appears to inspire a chemical reaction that makes us think and feel better. It's a dopamine thing. The concept of nicotine addiction was only put forward in the last two decades of the 20th century. One study has found that tobacco is as addictive as Class A drugs like heroin – or even more so – and is characterized by engendering a powerful urge to use it even when the effects are not as euphoric as rival illicit drugs. Many smokers try to quit and fail. Others live with the very real falsehood that they will give up smoking some time in the future. This is what makes smoking cigarettes so uniquely self-destructive.

In a legal argument against tobacco companies in Canada, the country's government insisted that nicotine was 'a drug, which just like cocaine and heroin, creates a strong addiction and which will kill one out of every two smokers'.

As in every other area of the smoking debate, there's an opposing view. Lauren A Colby, in his e-book *In Defence Of Smokers*, questions whether nicotine is the captivating ingredient in tobacco. 'If it were, nicotine patches should satisfy a smoker's craving for tobacco; they don't! In prisons, where, as a part of the punishment smoking is sometimes forbidden, the inmates take to smoking corn silk, paper, string, etc, none of which contain any nicotine.

'When I was a young man, there was a chain of tobacco stores which sold cheap cigars. They were made almost entirely from brown paper, with only one outside wrapper made from tobacco. I doubt they contained any significant amount of nicotine. Yet they were a satisfying smoke.'

If smoking is so bad for you, why isn't it banned? Smoking is legal, at least for adults, and the governments of the world show no inclination to change its status. Nicotine and alcohol are the two addictive drugs that society smiles upon. Their devotees are not hounded by the police or hauled in front of the courts while those who get their kicks from other drugs, including cannabis, heroin and cocaine, risk public admonition and imprisonment.

> 'Time takes a cigarette, puts it in your mouth/You pull on a finger, another finger, then a cigarette.' David Bowie, 'Rock 'n' Roll Suicide'

To some, the hypocrisy of it all is blatant. Is smoking pot so much worse than smoking cigarettes? Don't cigarettes kill many more people than heroin? Shouldn't every drug be banned? Maybe, but then there's such a thing as freedom of choice. There's an argument that says preventing people from smoking contravenes not only the American constitution but also the internationally recognized Human Rights Act. History has largely dictated the place of cigarettes in our society today and nothing much can change that.

Governments raise plenty of cash by placing inordinately high taxes upon cigarettes and there's a conflict between trade and health. Observers claim that that means law makers are disinclined to substantially reduce the number of smokers contributing to the state coffers. Savings in the costs of health provision for smokers don't match up to the income from cigarette sales and, the cynics insist, there's the added benefit of droves of people dying in their middle years and not requiring pensions, healthcare and so forth in old age. Smokers have been deprived of the right to see tobacco advertisements and, in some cases, they have been driven off the streets. But this has only happened recently while the nicotine war has been raging for 50 years.

> 'There's the social smoker who turns up at a party with a pack of ten and religiously smokes at least twice that amount. We call them "buy 10, smoke 12". "Why only 12?" I hear you ask. That's because they think that they've only smoked two more so it's therefore OK to keep buying packs of ten. We know different.' Jane Dennehy, marketing consultant, Line One

Whatever its motivation, government inaction appears to send mixed messages to smokers. In a survey by the British anti-smoking group ASH almost half of the smokers interviewed believed that smoking could not be all that bad. If it was, the British government would have at least banned advertising cigarettes and would consider an outright prohibition on smoking altogether.

'Half of all smokers still don't appreciate just how dangerous cigarettes are,' says John Connolly of ASH. 'The poll shows that the Government's actions (or lack of them) have an effect on how the public – especially smokers – perceive these risks.'

For today's tobacco manufacturers the situation is clear: individual choice is a fundamental right. According to British American Tobacco, 'Our business is not about persuading people to smoke; it is about offering quality brands to adults who have already taken the decision to smoke. We strongly believe that smoking should only be for adults who are aware of the risks.'

The Tobacco Manufacturers' Association is equally unequivocal on the subject: 'Smoking is an adult pursuit and should remain a matter for informed and adult choice.'

This brief pen portrait of the smoking scene is enough to tell you that there are plenty of reasons to smoke, and pressing ones not to. For perhaps the first time in history young people considering the option of smoking have the luxury of making an informed choice. The stakes are high and no one should light up without some of the swathes of statistics and analysis that are attached to the subject of smoking. Upon the importance of this, all sides are agreed.

CULTURE

Health educators pump out anti-smoking slogans just as fast as tobacco companies produce cartons of cigarettes. Both have the same target in focus: young would-be smokers.

For the health authorities it is imperative to hit young people with the 'don't smoke' message before they get started. Smoking is one of those troublesome conditions where prevention is far, far better than cure.

The tobacco industry stresses that it is interested solely in adult smokers and their spending power and not children. However, it is blatantly clear that cigarette companies are dependent on teenagers for their very survival. Let's be blunt: as older consumers die off it is vital to recruit new ones as replacements.

Tobacco companies are adamant that they are prepared to wait for young people to reach maturity before targeting them as customers – and have even put their money where they mouth is by financing Youth Smoking Prevention programmes. But, let's face it, the tobacco companies do not have the last word here. Successive surveys have shown that – regardless of tobacco industry policy or parental consent – 60 per cent of smokers have started by the age of 13 while just ten per cent adopt the habit after they have reached 20. At the moment it seems that the trend among teenagers to smoke remains steady or is rising.

Of course, young people are barred from buying cigarettes but that doesn't stop them either. Some 'borrow' from their parents' packets, others have friends working in sales outlets who buy on their behalf. There remains the possibility of buying cigarettes from vending machines. Some children lurk outside shops, asking strangers to make a purchase on their behalf. In the US there have been calls to raise the age limit to purchase cigarettes to 21.

According to Britain's Royal College of Physicians half of today's teenage smokers will die prematurely if they do not give up the habit now. 'One quarter will die in middle age, losing an average of 20 to 25 years of their lives and the other quarter will die in old age, losing an average of five to ten years of their lives,' said Dr John Britton, chair of the College's tobacco advisory group. 'We have reached a crisis point in the battle to save children from the greatest cause of death in the UK.'

Starting young means that lungs are exposed to years of smoke and so the risk of lung cancer increases. But this means little to the young Americans eager to get their fingers around bidis, hand-rolled on the streets of Delhi and the last word in cigarette style. Bidis are flavoured and hold particular appeal for the young. But research has revealed that they have to be puffed more frequently to keep them alight, and thus deliver three times as much nicotine and five times as much tar as regular cigarettes.

It's not all bad news. In Finland, Iceland, Italy, Slovenia and Sweden less than a quarter of the population aged 15 and over now smokes. Cigarette consumption in the United States is falling across the board and globally the number of cigarettes smoked per head of population is being driven down.

Image is key when it comes to smoking and cigarettes. Teenagers – with their hormones all haywire – are impressed with the apparent easy sophistication that comes with a cigarette. They are ready to believe that everyone who is anyone is smoking and that, to count, they must do so too. Not so, says the American Surgeon General who insists that although 3,000 children start smoking every day only 13 per cent of his country's adolescents have smoked in the last 30 days. Just eight per cent are frequent smokers.

However, peer pressure is pivotal in the decision to start smoking. Schoolmates who smoke always seem a class apart. All adolescents are aspirational adults and, for the young, smoking is a bridge into the grown-up world, illicitly enjoyed in the same way as alcopops, sodas laced with spirits. Cigarettes speak of confidence and independence, machismo among boys, femininity among girls. With smoking comes a strong identity that transcends IQ or background. Cigarette in hand, teenage smokers can sneer at the establishment, staging a one-man rebellion with a wave of their smoke-wreathed fingers.

As a Philip Morris marketing document explains, 'A cigarette for the beginner is a symbolic act. I am no longer my mother's child, I'm tough, I am an adventurer, I'm not square...'

So it seems devastatingly easy to stereotype young people who smoke: rebellious, charismatic, strident, sure of themselves. But this, it now appears, is somewhat misleading. Some of the recent research on the issue depicts young smokers as followers rather than leaders. Children who feel a need to define themselves with cigarette use often have poor self image and low personal esteem. They do not have the confidence to say no when someone offers them a smoke, believing it will make them less popular or credible. In America statistics have proved that children who smoke or chew tobacco are likely to turn in lower grades or be college drop-outs.

Nearly one in five men and one in ten women in the UK smoke more than 20 cigarettes a day.

The first cigarette is not always a happy experience. There are numerous reports of smokers feeling dizzy or sick, or even that their lungs are on fire. They also experience a 'head rush', caused by the effect of nicotine.

Jane Oxnam recalls her first – and last – cigarette, enjoyed at the Merchant Naval Officers Hostel in Plymouth, England: 'I was 15 and had drunk Guinness and whisky when somebody gave me a cigarette. I had somebody rather attractive lolling over me and I thought I looked cool.

'But later I was so copiously sick I blocked up a sink. I was unconscious for a while. After that I couldn't bear the smell of smoke nor could I bear the smell of whisky. I never touched either again. It's what they call an "ab reaction".'

Poet Adam Hamilton recently gave up smoking after 30 years of self-confessed addiction. 'I smoked my first cigarette aged about seven with a couple of mates. The first evidence of the link with cancer must have been in the air but, being kids, we'd obviously got hold of the wrong end of the stick because I remember us making bad jokes about how it could

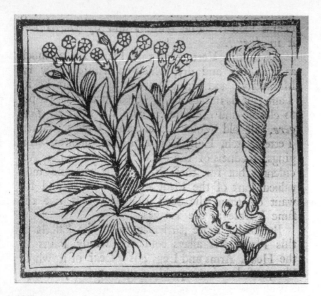

1690 engraving of a tobacco plant, *Nicotiana sp*, with a man smoking it (LOWER RIGHT), taken from a book in which it was claimed that tobacco 'may be said to be amongst the first rank among medicinal herbs, because of the singular vertues contained therein'. The tobacco plant is an annual or perennial shrub native to tropical America. It produces the toxic alkaloid nicotine to protect it from damage inflicted by grazing creatures. Tobacco smoking probably began amongst the Mayan peoples of Central America before the habit was taken to Europe in 1556.

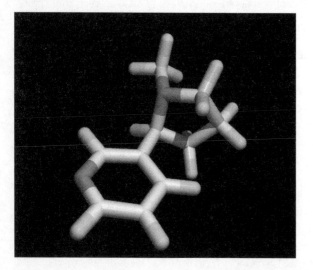

Molecular graphic of nicotine (formula $C_{10}H_{14}N_2$), an oily, colourless liquid, with the atoms here represented as sticks. Nicotine is the active component of tobacco, and in small doses it stimulates the autonomic nervous system, although tolerance builds up fast, leading to addiction. As well as the toxic effects of nicotine, smoking tobacco can also lead to serious lung problems, including cancer.

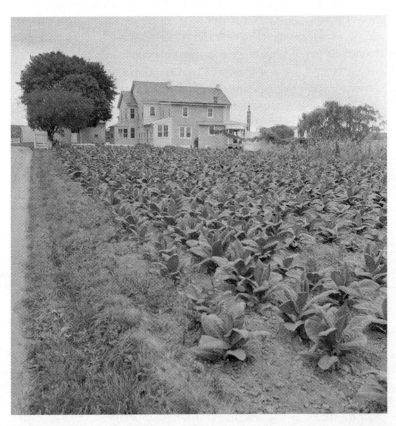

A tobacco field on an Amish farm in Lancaster County, Pennsylvania.

cause polio. The cigarette in question was a Woodbine. It tasted so disgusting that I wasn't tempted to repeat the experiment for at least another seven years.

'My next smoke was on a school trip. Peer pressure! By the age of 15 I was smoking five a day. We used to sneak off for a fag at break time. Our favourite place was by a dirty stream just outside the school grounds, though we would sometimes disappear into cupboards or storerooms within the school. A big part of the attraction of smoking was undoubtedly breaking school rules and the risk of getting caught –which could mean suspension or even expulsion.'

Nicholas Charles, who began smoking cigarettes at 11, was still a schoolboy when he decided to try pipe smoking 'to be like the man in the St Bruno [pipe tobacco] advertisement'.

'I bought a pipe and a tobacco pouch and cycled off into the countryside. Eventually I sat with my back against a tree, filled the pipe, lit it and began puffing away. It wasn't very long before I was sick over that tree, then I was sick again and again. I was sick twice more on the way home and I don't think I have ever felt as bad as I did that day.

'I had no idea that the technique for pipe smoking was a little different to cigarettes. I must have inflicted a massive nicotine overdose on myself, one that my system just could not tolerate even though I was already a smoker.' Charles avoided pipes for the rest of his days but indulged in cigarettes for a further half dozen years.

Tim Coulson, a marketing consultant who runs the company Line One, said, 'I had my first cigarette (in a friend's dog's kennel, aged seven – me, not the dog) but I didn't start seriously until I was 16 and at school. We built a smokers' hut called Piccadilly and thought we were really cool and that no one knew. The headmaster asked me if I wanted to be a prefect, but said that I'd have to give up smoking first. I was elated and devastated at the same time. How the hell did he know?'

One reason women and girls smoke is to suppress their appetites. They are, it seems, more weight conscious than health conscious. For some, a cigarette replaces a meal as smoking makes them feel less hungry. Ironically, it seems being bombarded with images of stick-thin females throughout the media fashions the outlook of women and girls – exposing them to the horrors of the 'slimmers' disease' anorexia nervosa – while overwhelming quantities of anti-smoking advice does not make one jot of difference to their point of view. As one wit pointed out, cigarette sales would plummet overnight if the packets bore the warning 'cigarettes contain fat'.

On average smokers weigh some 4kg less than non-smokers and that's because cigarettes not only help to suppress the appetite but also because nicotine affects the metabolic rate, making the body work faster and therefore use more calories. But any weight gain among those who have quit smoking tends to be temporary, the Royal College of Physicians has found: 'Quitting cigarette smoking is associated with an increase in appetite and caloric intake, with a subsequent weight gain over six to 12 months. Thereafter, both caloric intake and weight return to baseline.'

The big picture indicates that obesity remains on the increase, too, so the overall effectiveness of a cigarette in reducing appetite appears largely ineffective. What's more, current research says that smoking might stem a rampant appetite but it also changes the weight distribution on a woman, altering the hip-to-waist ratio. In effect, women smokers are likely to end up with pot bellies and spindly legs.

In the US the Surgeon General David Satcher's report on women and smoking in 2001 promised that lung cancer would kill nearly 68,000 American women that year, representing one in every four cancer deaths in the country. It outstripped breast cancer as a killer by as many as 27,000 cases. The full story was even worse, with about 165,000 women dying prematurely in 1999 through smoking-related diseases.

'When calling attention to public health problems we must not misuse the word "epidemic". But there is no better word to describe the 600 per cent increase since 1950 in women's deaths from lung cancer, a disease primarily caused by cigarette smoking. Clearly, smoking-related disease among women is a full-blown epidemic,' wrote Satcher. And according to the Royal College of Physicians, 'Cigarette smoking shortens life expectancy at age

35 years for women by six years, compared with a woman who has never smoked cigarettes.'

Yet smoking has long been indelibly associated with liberation. For decades cigarette smoking among high-born women was frowned upon. As notions of sex equality spread among women, so did the desire to smoke. In the early 1800s smoking was confined to Parisienne prostitutes lurking in the vicinity of Notre Dame. Although cigarette smoking among women of all classes appeared acceptable in Paris by the middle of the 19th century, there was resistance to it elsewhere.

> 'We estimate that in 1997 cigarette smoking accounted for the loss of 205,000 years of life under age 65 and 551,000 years of life under age 75.' Royal College of Physicians

In the last half of the 19th century, Dr Russell Thacher Trall wrote, 'Some of the ladies of this refined and fashion-forming metropolis [New York] are aping the silly ways of some pseudo-accomplished foreigners, in smoking tobacco through a weaker and more feminine article, which has been most delicately denominated "cigarette".'

As late as 1896 London society was scandalized when the Duchess de Clermont Tonnerre smoked a cigarette in the dining room of the Savoy Hotel. Although old women from the lower classes smoked 'as a solace and a comfort' in preference to drinking, Victorian Britain still wanted its aristocratic women demure – and smoking scarcely fitted the image.

Pansy Montague, a daring Australian show girl with the stage name 'La Milo' who was a hit in Edwardian London, put her name to a brand of cigarettes. As infamous for her diaphanous robes as for her connection with smoking, a whiff of sensationalism clung to her as it did to all women who smoked.

But times were changing. In 1908 a woman columnist for Australian *Punch* observed, 'Fragrance of lavender, scent of rose-leaves, are not the only perfumes which cling to ladies' boudoirs. The cigarette habit has apparently come to stay. Little smoking is done in public. Our women have not attained the Continental disregard for worn-out conventions. In Paris and London it is "the thing" to smoke unabashed, provided you have got over the splutter and choking stage.'

The topic of whether women should smoke and if men should see them do it became the subject of lively debate. Still, before the 1920s women who smoked were generally thought to be shocking and 'loose'. Railway commissioners in Australia ordered ladies-only smoking carriages to be designed, out of consideration for men who did not like the company of ladies when smoking.

There was concern, too, that willowy women smoking to conserve calories were risking consumption, which was once a killer disease. With remarkable foresight, one Dr JS Russell reported to the Institute of Hygiene in February 1926 that women were becoming ravaged by a lifestyle riddled with tobacco and alcohol.

'Scarcely has the age of 20 been reached before the lines that belong to the face of a woman of middle age become evident in such girls.'

In the same year the Religious Tract Society was moved to warn women against the use of cigarettes for fear that perpetual puckering would cause moustaches to grow on their upper lips.

But the cigarette makers, spying a new, untapped market, were beginning to seize the day. A Marlboro advertisement launched in 1925 smashed the stereotype by asking, 'Has smoking any more to do with a woman's morals than has the colour of her hair?' The connection between women's freedom and smoking was firmly planted in the minds of the public in a series of advertising campaigns conducted over decades. Among the most memorable are those for Virginia Slims, comparing a bold, beautiful woman smoking openly next to a sepia image of a secret smoker of yesteryear. 'You've come a long way, baby' is the message. Even now it is difficult to shake off the idea that cigarettes represent independence.

> 'Cigarettes are the only substance sold that, when the user follows the instructions carefully, will result in the consumer becoming toxic, chronically ill or dead!' Dr Max Snyder in his documentary *The Medical Aspects Of Tobacco*

Today women choose to smoke for many different reasons. For Yvonne Casey it is all about taking time out to appreciate the good things in life. 'A lot of people are tension smokers but for me it is all about relaxing. There is nothing like smoking on a beach at sunset or on a hilltop with a glorious view, with all that pure air. I love to get a cigarette out of the packet, put it between my fingers and strike a match – I never use lighters. The smell of the match and the feel of the cigarette, it is quite glamorous. It is the first puff that is the main thing. I could throw it away after that or just sit and hold the cigarette until it is finished.

'When I have been in the company of a heavy smoker and smoked a lot I feel dreadful afterwards, terribly unhealthy and sure that I have done for myself. I feel guilty for doing something as ridiculous as smoking but that guilt is overcome by the beauty of it.'

A mother of three, Yvonne confines herself to social smoking and often 'borrows' cigarettes at parties. 'People have never minded, they rather like the fact that somebody else smokes. They are relieved that they are not a leper on their own.'

Although her husband is a non-smoker, her daughter, a dancer, also smokes. 'It is typical among dancers to smoke,' explained Casey. 'As soon as she got to dancing college she and her class mates were lectured about the dangers of smoking. Nobody took the slightest bit of notice.' One son, a keen sportsman, has never smoked while the other gave up his habit of social smoking at the Millennium.

Some women choose to smoke because it is a stress-buster. Helen South smoked from the age of 15. 'There were no side effects at all,' she says. 'I was hooked straight away.' But although she has stopped smoking for long periods, including three pregnancies, she has no intention of giving up at the moment. 'I don't want to give up because I don't want to inflict myself on my family. When I'm not smoking I am terribly crabby. I snap. Smoking makes me calm when I am naturally a nervous person.'

Stress led another 41-year-old woman back to smoking years after she first kicked the habit. 'After my separation I started to go out with a group of younger people who smoked and I started to do it as a social thing. As the stress of dealing with the custody battle for my children increased I found I would smoke more and more although I hadn't been a smoker for years.

'People told me I was mad to start smoking and I kept saying I'd give up but couldn't get around to it. Finally, when my young son went to stay with his best friend, the boy's mother said the bedroom stank of smoke from my son's pyjamas and I realized how sad that was. My own child stank because of me. I gave up then and never looked back.'

One woman described the attraction of smoking like this: 'It is not the nicotine that makes me smoke. It's the feeling I get of "just blow the lot of them". When I smoke, I smoke for me and I can put aside the demands of children, husband, and work.'

It is a similar principle that applies to poorer people who smoke in order to take precious moments out of a mundane job or deprived living conditions.

Statistically smoking is still a habit that belongs to the disadvantaged in society. While wealthy people tend to kick the habit the poor keep getting poorer through smoking. The Royal College of Physicians outlined the situation in Britain. 'In relation to occupation in 1996 smoking prevalence was lowest in the professional (12 per cent) and highest in the semi-skilled manual occupation groups (39 per cent).

'Other measures of relative poverty or deprivation, including housing tenure, crowding, living in rented accommodation, being divorced or separated, unemployment, low education achievement and, in women, single parent status, are also independently associated with an increased risk of smoking amongst adults.

'Analysis of trends in smoking based on a composite index of some of these measures indicates that over the period 1973 to 1996 smoking prevalence fell by more than 50 per cent in the most advantaged sector of British society but has remained unchanged in the most deprived group.'

Despite the dangers of smoking, there has been a deafening silence about them in those women's magazines that also advertise cigarettes. A study conducted in 1997 and 1998 in America of 13 women's magazines covering 130 different editions found that less than one per cent of health-related articles were devoted to anti-smoking messages. Only one out of 519 health-related features concerned smoking while 53 articles centred on nutrition. This is a cause for concern as literally millions of readers look forward to delivery of their chosen magazine and even rely on it for relevant health information.

The fear is, of course, that magazines will upset advertisers in their editorials although most journalists would strenuously deny this was the case. The topic of smoking is an old chestnut and the anti-smoking argument needs something new and fresh to attract publicity, they would argue. Dr Elizabeth Whelan, from the American Council on Science and Health (ACSH), describes the coverage as 'glaringly scant'. She is also concerned about the mixed message emerging from women's magazines that condemn smoking on one page while apparently condoning it by housing advertising for it on another.

One of the most pressing reasons cited by women for quitting smoking is the effect it has on the complexion. There's no doubt that smoking has an ageing effect. For years the evidence that smoking made people appear older than their years was primarily anecdotal. It was widely assumed that smokers bore more wrinkles because they were perpetually squinting through a smoke haze. In 2001 a team at the St John's Institute of Dermatology in London revealed that smoking activates the genes responsible for an enzyme in the skin which attacks collagen, the protein which gives it elasticity. Once the collagen is broken down the skin becomes loose and wrinkly. Women could be faced with the colossal costs of anti-ageing cream when possibly the best remedy would be to give up smoking.

> 'I thought I couldn't afford to take her out and smoke as well, so I gave up cigarettes. Then I took her out and one day I looked at her and thought, "Oh well," and I went back to smoking again, and that was better.' Comedian Benny Hill

This fact could be crucial in the battle for hearts and minds in the arena of smoking. At the moment anti-smoking campaigns are experiencing a lamentable lack of success in persuading young girls in particular and young people in general to say no to cigarettes.

A recent report into smoking in Europe conducted by the World Health Organization revealed that there was no significant reduction in the numbers of young people smoking despite the abundance of health warnings directed at them.

Teenage girls are smoking as much as boys when traditionally they have smoked less. The figure stands at about 30 per cent across east and west Europe. The same study revealed that girls smoke more than adult women, flagging up problems in years to come. Given the vulnerability of young people, the Royal College of Physicians remains concerned at why so many fall into the 'trap' of smoking.'Young people do not always have the capacity to make informed decisions and society generally recognizes this by providing greater protection for children than for adults.

'In the case of tobacco, the problem of immature decision making is compounded by nicotine addiction. Decisions to smoke made in the early teens can be consolidated into addictive behaviour before the smoker reaches maturity.'

The first World No-Tobacco Day was held in 1988, sponsored by the World Health Organization. Its impact on juvenile smokers, however, seems to have been negligible.

In fact, children are for the most part many generally bitterly opposed to cigarettes and smoking, according to Simon Clark is the director of Forest, an organization that describes itself as the 'voice and friend of the smoker'. 'Our limited experience of speaking to children about smoking is that, until the age of 13, 99 per cent of children think it is terrible for you and promise to go home and tell their parents not to smoke. Then there is a sea change at about 14 when a considerable number start smoking. It is a form of rebellion.

'As an organization we try to avoid the whole subject of under 16s smoking as it is an emotional issue. We do not want to see children smoking. We would support most initiatives to discourage children from smoking. We are here to support an adult's right to choose and children are used as a stick to beat adults about the head with on this issue.

'We do think some of the anti-smoking campaigns are counter productive. They are a form of nagging'.

Some anti-smoking campaigns are hard-hitting and controversial. Clark is sceptical about the power of such tactics. He believes the increasingly emotive language and vivid analogies of the 'antis' are self-defeating.

'In the past year I have heard campaigners talk of a cigarette being the equivalent of a dirty syringe used by heroin addicts. Parents who smoke have been called child abusers.

. 'Ordinary smokers switch off when they hear this because none of them compare themselves with heroin addicts. There is no evidence that people who smoke go around mugging old ladies to pay for their so-called addiction. Heroin is a mind-altering substance. There is no suggestion that smoking is mind-altering.

'Likewise, on an average Friday or Saturday night, it is alcohol not nicotine that is responsible for hospital casualty departments being rather busier than usual.

'Anti-smoking campaigners say "quit or die". It is very black and white. The reality is there are a lot of grey areas. For example, there are a lot of people who live to a rich old age who have been life-long smokers. They have not had a day's ill health related to smoking. Some people smoke because they enjoy it. There are many anti-smoking campaigners who cannot believe anyone can enjoy smoking – but they do. Quit or die is too stark.'

Author and BBC radio panellist Claire Fox cut her daily cigarette consumption from 40 to two. But national initiatives like 'No-Smoking Day' played no part in her decision: 'Last year, as I mulled over giving up, the No-Smoking Day stunts and media profile infuriated rather than inspired me. There's something about the moralistic tone of the no-smoking campaigns that makes a lot of us want to reach for our fags in defiance. It took me a long time to really try to give up. Ironically one of the main reasons for this was the increasingly moralistic tone of official anti-smoking campaigns over recent years. I don't like being hectored, lectured at or treated like a naughty child for having a habit (not an addiction), the risks and disadvantages of which I am well aware.

'Being a smoker has also meant being treated as a pariah. Smokers of the UK have huddled outside offices, been squeezed out of restaurants and social gatherings, been blamed for asthma and cancer in non-smokers, been accused of wasting National Health Service resources by self-inflicted illness. But this demonization has backfired. The solidarity of rebellion has meant that many people have carried on smoking regardless. In fact

– if being a smoker meant a poke in the eye to the new puritans – all the more reason to light up.'

Adam Hamilton tries to rationalize why smoking remains popular despite the hazards it presents. 'I find that the more smokers are vilified the more attractive they appear. I grew up at a time when smoking was sexy and cool. A lot of it was bound up with the louche, warts'n'all humanity of rebels and anti-heroes from Humphrey Bogart to Jean-Paul Belmondo and Bob Dylan. The associations of smoking are definitely part of the allure – the smoky atmosphere of nightclubs, offering a cigarette or a light to someone you fancy... My favourite cigarette – and the hardest one for me to renounce – was the evening one, with coffee, after a good meal with wine.

'As an adult smoker I continued to enjoy the conspiratorial "bike-shed" aspect of smoking. As "no-smoking" environments proliferated, I found that enjoying a crafty fag was the beginning of many a beautiful friendship. At least one networking session, leading to a crucial business deal, began on the balcony of a no-smoking building.'

Marketing consultant Jane Dennehy has also enjoyed the feeling of belonging to a 'club' that smoking creates. 'In the years that I have smoked I have noticed certain personality types associated with smoking. Of course I am taking for granted the fact that at boring events if you nip out for a smoke you usually find sociable people doing the same thing, it's almost a secret club. These are the real smokers, the diehards who like me take the whole habit pretty seriously and adhere to the unspoken rules.'

'Smokers are so often made to feel like social pariahs, often the best "craic" can be found with the other rule breakers,' says Tim Coulson. 'That's why you'll always find us outside the kitchen at parties!'

Geoff Lawson, the headteacher of Christleton High School in Chester, tried to eliminate the 'bike shed' culture of smoking by introducing supervised smoking breaks. Pupils who signed up for the scheme were then involved in regular sessions to educate themselves about the dangers the habit presented. In addition, smokers were assigned non-smoking 'buddies' to help them break the habit. The aim was to rid the school toilets of smokers and therefore cut the risk of passive smoking for the remainder of the school population. Initially the results were promising, said Lawson,

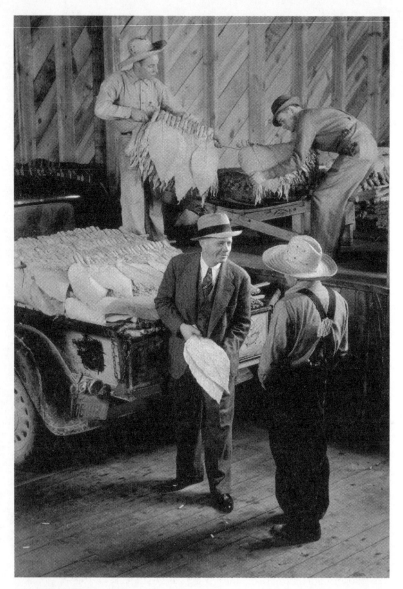

American businessman speaking with a tobacco farmer in a storage barn, 1940. Two farmhands are loading leaves onto a truck.

Italian explorer Christopher Columbus (1451–1506) is widely believed to have discovered the New World and the tobacco plant growing there. Tobacco leaves and seeds were brought back to Europe after his 1492 foray, having been presented to him by Arawak Indians in the West Indies, but it was his companion Rodrigo de Jerez who was the first white man to smoke regularly. He was allegedly reported to the Inquisition for his habit by someone who believed that he was Satanically possessed and was released from prison only after smoking became widespread in Spain.

English explorer and adventurer Sir Francis Drake (c1540–96), who took to the high seas more than 50 years after the Columbus's death, forming relations with the Miwok Indians on America's Pacific coast, where he most likely developed a taste for tobacco.

Painting by Jean Leon Gerome Ferris depicting Native American Princess Pocahontas (1595–1617) at the time of her marriage to colonialist John Rolfe (1585–1622). Rolfe helped bring about the mass cultivation of tobacco at an early stage in the history of Virginia, experimenting with seeds and yields and importing new varieties from the West Indies.

King James I of England (1566–1625), tobacco's most famous opponent, as portrayed in a painting by Van Dyck. Alerted to the expanding use of tobacco by physicians, its use by people without prescription, and its possible association with witchcraft, in 1604 James issued an edict called *A Counterblaste To Tobacco* in which he wrote, 'Smoking is a custom loathsome to the eye, hateful to the nose, harmful to the brain, dangerous to the lungs, and in the black, stinking fume thereof nearest resembling the horrible Stygian smoke of the pit that is bottomless.'

but long school holidays dented the success of the scheme. He felt that shocking images of the bodily havoc caused by cigarettes turned many smokers into quitters. Parents were largely supportive of bringing young smokers into the open.

British American Tobacco accepts it is on something of a knife-edge where teen smoking is concerned. 'We view youth smoking as a critical issue in today's society, and want to help ensure that only informed adults smoke. We fully support laws and regulations on a minimum age for buying tobacco products and penalties for retailers who break the law. Our company policy world wide is not to market to anyone under 18 years old, or higher if the law in a particular country sets the age higher,' explained a spokesman.

'Although some people are critical of the involvement of tobacco companies in efforts against youth smoking, we believe that to do nothing or not to get involved is not an option. In many countries where no other organizations are able or prepared to support such initiatives, tobacco company YSP programmes are often the only programmes in the country.

'There is no "right" way to develop a YSP programme and one programme will not fit all countries. Our prevention programmes are increasingly based on research into current attitudes as well as building on existing experience. Over time this enables us to identify the most effective aspects of programmes and any weaknesses, which in turn helps us develop best practice.'

One of the most successful anti-smoking campaigns in America is orchestrated by Patrick Reynolds, a grandson of the tobacco company founder RJ Reynolds. He turned against smoking after witnessing the death of his father and eldest brother from smoking-related diseases. Now he tours the country delivering a hard-hitting lecture about the perils of smoking.

In it, Reynolds highlights the story of Sean Marsee, an accomplished athlete who began chewing tobacco in his mid-teens. Soon he was addicted and attempts by his mother, a nurse, to make him quit failed. One day Sean showed his mother a lump that had appeared on his tongue. It turned out to be cancer. An operation to remove the lump failed to rid his body of the disease. It spread to his jaw and neck muscles and finally, aged 19, Sean died, disfigured and in pain. Reynolds goes on to look at tobacco company tactics, the nature of addiction, the potency of cigarette advertisements and the science of smoking.

Like other anti-smoking campaigns, the lecture is full of merit. But none of the anti-smoking campaigners answer the question about why so many young people choose to smoke. Jonjo O'Neill, 18, has smoked since the age of 12 when he took his first, illicit puff with a group of pals. 'My friends and I clubbed our money together and bought a packet of cigarettes. We smoked them in a field. I didn't inhale properly so I wasn't sick. It wasn't peer pressure. I'm always interested in doing something I'm not supposed to. Now I smoke about 15 a day.'

O'Neill is convinced he will not be a lifelong smoker. 'I will give up when I finish university. I know I'm addicted but I do it to pass the time. I smoke a whole lot more at college because we get breaks when there is absolutely nothing to do except have a cigarette. I know a couple of people who have started smoking since they have come to college through boredom. I suppose part of the reason I light up is to get rid of the tension smoking creates. A cigarette relaxes me but only because I need the nicotine. It is the effect on my health that bothers me, I don't care what other people think.'

Julian Cann, 19, was also 12 when he first smoked a roll-up. 'I wasn't that impressed. But I've smoked on and off since then. I will never be a full-on smoker. I know it is bad for me and I accept the risks. But I don't think there should be advertisements or sponsorship to promote cigarettes. Tobacco companies don't really have to advertise because once people are addicted they are always going to buy.'

'Lots of girls are smoking because cigarettes are known to be a hunger suppressant and everyone wants to be skinny,' explains Gillian Reitz, 16, who smoked her first − and last − cigarette at a party. 'They think it makes them look cool and their friends are all doing it. Personally I thought it was disgusting. It tasted horrible and it made me feel sick. I took it so no one could accuse me of being a hypocrite, by saying I don't like smoking when I had never ever tried it. But I don't think I'll try it again.'

Philip Hope, 18, smoked a single cigarette at the age of 15. 'It didn't really do anything for me, that is why I didn't take it up. I smoked it because of peer pressure, and because I liked the thought of trying something I hadn't tried before. But I just couldn't see the point of it. A lot of my friends smoke. I expect they could give it up if they tried, they do it more for fashion than anything else. The cost of cigarettes isn't a problem.

'But I think it smells horrible, not just when you do it yourself but when you have been with people who do it.'

Chris Freeman, 17, has decided to quit smoking. 'I said to myself I would start today so that is what I'm doing. I might as well start sometime. I'm going to do it with will power. If that doesn't work I'm going to go on to patches.'

A sporty young man with ambitions to join the navy, he has become concerned over how smoking has affected his health. 'I want to regain my fitness. When I first began my college course I ran a mile and a half in 9.40 minutes. Six months later I ran the same distance in 13.16 minutes. During that time I had got a job and began to earn enough money to pay for cigarettes.'

At 17, Gina Pope has already started – and quit – smoking. Like many young people she gave up even before she reached the legal age to buy a packet of cigarettes. Her big concerns were the health issues related to smoking but she can recall the days when she was a regular purchaser of a packet. 'I don't smoke now because I like to play football. Smoking is bad for your health and it is not all it is cracked up to be. But I used to empty my piggy bank and take 2d's and 1d's into a local garage to buy cigarettes when I was about 13. It was obvious that I was under age, but they still served me.'

'"Don't smoke" is advice hard for patients to swallow. May we suggest instead "Smoking Philip Morris?" Tests showed three out of every four cases of smokers' cough cleared on changing to Philip Morris. Why not observe the results for yours?' Advert placed in the US *National Medical Journal For Doctors*, 1943

Some young people base their decisions about smoking on tragic personal experience. Chris Edmonds, 18, explained, 'I have never smoked. My nan died when she was 65 years old. She smoked all her life. She was killed by emphysema and in the end she had an oxygen machine in the house. Her mother outlived her by four years. I thought to myself, "I don't want to live like that at all." I don't mind if people smoke, it is their life. But I won't.'

Donna Brady, 17, thinks fewer people would smoke if only their skin was transparent. 'If people could see what it was doing to their organs it would be a major deterrent. It is pretty horrible. Young people smoke because they are bored or because their family and friends smoke. Maybe there's an image issue as well.'

Robbie Holtom, 19, is, frankly, baffled by the continuing attraction of smoking. 'I can't find any reason why people should smoke when there are obviously such dire consequences. It is totally bizarre.

'I played a lot of sport at school and all of us were really anti-smoking because it does affect your per-formance on the field. Two people did smoke. They thought it was really cool. They were told by teachers if they did not stop smoking they would be out of the rugby team. They did give up – for the rugby season.

'It is a bit like standing in front of a bonfire and breathing in the smoke. Why would you do it?

'I'll endorse with my name any of the following: clothing, AC/DC, cigarettes, small tapes, sound equipment, rock 'n' roll records, anything – film and film equipment, food, helium, whips, money!'
Andy Warhol

'I did A-level biology and we looked at lungs that had been affected through smoking. They were blackened and blotchy and really nasty. Yet there were smokers among us who shrugged it off, saying, "That is going to happen much later on in life." And these were really intelligent people.

'I wouldn't go out with a girl who smoked. I don't like the smell of people who smoke. Fortunately none of my close friends smoke. In our school year of about 70 there were only three who smoked. But in the year below it was many more.'

'Smoking kills you,' says 12-year-old Lewis Constable. 'I want to be a footballer and the only way to get there is not to smoke. People start smoking because they think it is cool. It is the action of sucking on a cigarette and particularly blowing out. I don't think it is cool to kill yourself. People have offered me cigarettes in the past but I turn them down. I don't feel awkward about it, I just don't want to know.'

To 'protect' boys like Lewis cigarettes have been banned for years from the advertising opportunities of hoardings or television. Some witty and clever admen's handiwork has thus been consigned to history although the best jingles remain in the brain years later.

Yet research is telling us that the limited advertising available to manufacturers still has an effect. There are claims that Joe Camel, the character created to market Camel cigarettes, is as familiar to children as Mickey Mouse.

Sport has been one of the largest benefactors of the tobacco companies' enormous revenues, distributed in the form of sponsorship. Motor racing, cricket, rallying, snooker and even athletics have been scooping them in. For fervent anti-smokers, the association with sport has been one of the most loathsome and pernicious forms of marketing in the world today. They believe sports events and stadia reek of health and clean living while the odour of disease clings inescapably to cigarettes.

Undoubtedly, and almost by osmosis, children absorb the brand names promoted by sports sponsorship and can readily identify them when it comes to choosing a first cigarette. The cigarette and notions of athletic excellence become linked in their minds. For this reason, some professional sports teams or outlets have taken the decision to ban smoking advertisements from their stadia.

Tobacco sponsorship and advertising has been shuffled to the sidelines for years, mostly by way of voluntary codes. But now legislation is being brought in everywhere designed to stop sponsorship and adverts by tobacco firms.

The British government is banning all tobacco advertising. By doing so it believes it will help save 3,000 lives, reducing the number of deaths caused each year by smoking by 2.5 per cent. Clearly it believes the potency of advertising is great, especially among the young. Alan Millburn, the Health Secretary who backed a ban on tobacco advertising, comments, '[It] is a tough but proportionate response to the marketing and promotion of the only legally available product which kills one in two of its regular, long-term users.'

His actions were backed by Sir Richard Doll, one of the scientists to first link lung cancer with smoking, who feels such measures are long overdue. 'Smoking doesn't give much pleasure. It is a habit until you become addicted to the nicotine. It has been very disappointing that the government has taken so little action and has allowed promotion of tobacco to continue for 50 years [since the first links with lung cancer were made]. It was 25 years before they started increasing taxation on cigarettes for health purposes. The failure of successive governments to abolish the promotion of smoking, which is so dangerous that it doubles the risk of dying, is disappointing and quite extraordinary.'

'The tobacco industry has been very aggressive in its attempts to make the world believe that tobacco products are harmless and need not be regulated but it is obvious that people just don't buy their arguments,' says Dr Derek Yach, executive director of Noncommunicable Diseases at the World Health Organization. 'People, as well as governments, know that the best protection from tobacco lies in strong regulation.'

As writer Mark Asher points out, 'You have to question where those revenues have gone now. Third World sponsorship, perhaps, where laws are either more relaxed or non-existent.'

To appreciate the pulling power of an advertisement, look no further than 'Marlboro man'. Evolving from the marketing strategies drawn up at makers Philip Morris, 'Marlboro man' was a physical Adonis who bore just the right amount of stubble, casual yet chic and rugged yet wise. He was the cowboy that every adolescent dreamed of being. He was the free spirit that every girl wanted to tame. (I should mention here that one of the models for 'Marlboro man' died of lung cancer.)

However, the dangers of tobacco advertising and promotion may have been over-played. Jane Dennehy recalls that her first cigarette was linked, not to advertising, but to playing sport. 'I can't remember taking up smoking but I know it was around the time I started playing serious netball. Any connection with sport? No. Any connection with sponsorship? Definitely not because there wasn't any.'

Clearly impervious to advertising, she added, 'All I can say about my early days of smoking was that I started on one brand and have never deviated, not even when desperate – and never menthol.'

Tim Coulson agrees: 'I've tried lots of brands but for the past few years I've been pretty loyal. I have to say that I have never been influenced by advertising towards any particular brand. Smokers tend to change only if offered an alternative to their usual brand and if they like the taste.'

The issue about whether tobacco advertising should be permitted at all remains contentious. The World Health Organization insists that no country has yet succeeded in drawing up regulations that give tobacco advertising an 'adult-only' perimeter. All tobacco advertising can be seen by children and, after all, what brick walls can be built to allow a 19-year-old to see cigarette slogans while preventing a 17-year-old from doing so?

Even the tobacco industry itself is doubtful that advertising makes a difference. Advertising campaigns conducted in the past have thrown up no evidence of expanding sales. Indeed, sometimes it can have the opposite effect. Advertisements are designed to reinforce brand values, to introduce new brands or to invite smokers to switch brands. It can be argued that non-smokers are hardly likely to light up for the first time on seeing an advertising billboard, nor are existing smokers poised to consume cigarettes in greater numbers. When events are sponsored by drinks manufacturers it doesn't appear to correlate into a swelling in the number of alcoholics. But perhaps the primary function of advertising tobacco products is that it can give tobacco products social acceptability at a time when health agencies are trying to strip it of that quality.

> In 1999 1.6 trillion cigarettes were consumed in China, compared with 415 billion in the United States.

In the past the government has hammered out a mutual agreement with the tobacco industry on how it advertises and promotes its products. Disappointed by the British government's recourse to law, the industry has always believed that these voluntary agreements worked well and were the best option. For example, in January 1995, guidelines prevented tobacco advertising from appearing in publications aimed wholly or mainly at people under the age of 18. In addition, advertising was banned from magazines with women readers between the ages of 15 and 24. Permanent shop front advertising was phased out while any posters within sight of a school or college were banned. All of which adds up to a responsible, well-thought-out piece of legislation. The number of instances when the guidelines were contravened was extremely small.

The role of cigarettes as a statement of the chic, couth and cosmopolitan can be found in books and films, and their inclusion seems justified. The archly urbane Commander James Bond favoured Morland Specials, bearing three gold rings. This was made to his own specification from Virginian and Balkan tobacco at a London tobacconist. He disliked held-out lighters and generally insisted on lighting his own. His creator, author Ian Fleming, knew his character's smoking habits down to the last detail – indeed, Bond's cigarette consumption somewhat mirrored that of Fleming. When he was with the CIA out of range of his tobacconist, Bond chose Chesterfields as an alternative. He was, according to one health report, a 60-a-day man.

Bond emerged on the silver screen in an era when the threat of cigarettes was beginning to make headlines. The fact that he smoked at all made him more alluringly dangerous while an uncommon number of his enemies abstained from the weed. Smoking was still a glamorous business and it seemed perfectly in keeping with his character that he should indulge. However, times have changed: leading man Pierce Brosnan persuaded Bond film makers to ditch the cigarettes in the most recent movies. Brosnan, who had once advertised Lark cigarettes, was convinced smoking was damaging to health and being seen on the big screen might have a ripple effect. His instincts, it seems, were all correct.

> 'Tobacco kills one person every ten seconds and is set to kill ten million people a year by 2025.' World Health Organization

Although research has shown that the sight of cigarettes in the hands and on the lips of film actors has increased four-fold recently, it does not guarantee healthy box-office returns. Kevin Costner's *Waterworld*, for example, showed no fewer than 121 cigarettes. It's probably a coincidence, but the film flopped.

However, the amount of smoking seen in films is significant, academics insist. One study claimed that children who saw a lot of smoking on the big screen were six times more likely to take up the habit.

The study, of 4,919 American schoolchildren aged between nine and 15, revealed that those who saw 50 or fewer screen stars smoking took up the habit at a rate of less than five per cent. Of those subjected to 150 snatches of film stars smoking, a sizeable 31.5 per cent tried smoking. (Alterations were made for social factors and demographic changes.) This could be because seeing larger-than-life characters puffing on a cigarette makes smoking seem the norm. Anti-smoking groups have called for censors to notch up the certificates on films featuring young heartthrobs fag-in-hand.

John Connolly, of ASH, says, 'These young people may be copying their favourite stars' smoking or they might be more likely to watch movies which make them feel comfortable about smoking, but either way it suggests that smoking on screen nurtures and sustains smoking among teenage movie fans – and everybody should be worried about that.

Dr Stan Glantz, of SmokeFreeMovies in the US, is even more explicit. 'In the last year's American movies, the amount of smoking has about doubled and the American movies have become the main pro-tobacco influence in many parts of the world. What I'm saying is that Hollywood needs to stop doing the tobacco industry's dirty work.'

While he would like to see cigarettes kept out of films, he realizes that there is credence in film industry claims that they are sometimes necessary for the purposes of realism (who would expect a World War II film not to feature smokers?).

However, he wants to see brands left unidentified, a film which features smoking to have an anti-smoking advertisement among the preceding trailers and also an announcement at the end of the film to the effect that no one was paid for placing the cigarette in the film. This kind of disclaimer is included in a film when animal cruelty appears to have happened on screen. Most actors and actresses are, he says, capable of transmitting emotions like tension, grief and notions of rebellion without the prop of a cigarette.

However, Todd Field, director of *In The Bedroom*, a film singled out by Glantz for its use of cigarettes, believes the use of generic cigarettes in films is 'asinine'.

Going one step further, 1995 saw the release of *Smoke*, starring William Hurt and Harvey Keitel, which chose for its core subject the goings-on among customers at a cigar shop and paid no heed to the sensibilities of the anti-smoking lobby. The shop owner played by Keitel is rarely seen without a cigarette between his fingers. In dialogue he makes no bones about the way he sees smoking law heading in America. 'Enjoy yourself while you can, man,' he tells a customer who is concerned about a possible prohibition on cigars. 'Tobacco today, sex tomorrow. In three or four years it will probably be against the law to smile at strangers.' Keitel represents the view of smokers who feel tobacco control is an infringement on liberty.

> 'The Institute and this publication believe that the American people want and are entitled to accurate, factual, interesting information about this business [tobacco] which is so important in the economic bloodstream of the nation and such a tranquillizer in our personal lives.'
> Statement to launch *Tobacco News*

The silver screen has become a tempting option for cigarette companies who are being squeezed out of traditional advertising spaces. There's evidence that they have spent thousands of dollars placing cigarettes in major films although observers believe that payments to directors and stars ended by the mid-1990s. The ending of such payments does not appear to have reduced the number of times that cigarettes have appeared in films.

But let's not overlook an alternative way in which cigarettes are used by the screen media. In *The Simpsons*, the well-loved cartoon, Marje's sisters Patti and Selma are portrayed as heavy smokers. Both are distinctly unsavoury characters – indeed, the Simpson children are repelled by the gravel-voiced sisters. They are reflecting the responses of many children who recoil from the embrace of a smoky older relative. There's nothing here that glamorizes cigarettes.

The blockbusting film *Lord Of The Rings* contains some spellbinding images involving smoking. Pipe-puffing Bilbo Baggins issues some large and strangely beautiful smoke rings which are in turn intercepted by smoky circles from the mouth of the wizard Gandalf. But at the sight of it will impressionable young people seek to become hobbits? Baggins's use of a pipe and the blowing of smoke rings was, of course, to suggest another era and another world rather than glamorize the activity.

Portrait of Charles II (1630–85), King of England and Scotland. When he was restored to the British throne, in 1660, he brought with him the French predilection for snuff.

1780s etching copied from of a work by the Dutch painter Adrian Ostades (1610–85) showing a man holding a pipe used for smoking tobacco.

Artwork, dating from the early 19th century, of a well-dressed man offering his companion snuff. Snuff is, strictly speaking, any drug prepared as a fine powder, administered by sniffing, and absorbed by the nasal membranes, although it is more commonly understood as finely powdered tobacco. It was originally used by Native Americans and imported into Europe during the 17th century, reaching the height of its popularity in the French court of the late 18th century. The search for ever more savage blends led to the addition of powdered pepper in later years.

In France, at least, the film industry has embraced something of a revolution as regards smoking. One of the most famous French films ever, *À Bout De Souffle* or *Breathless*, made in 1959 was filmed in a brooding smoke haze. The story is of a young car thief, Jean-Paul Belmondo, who kills a policeman and goes on the run with his American girlfriend, Jean Seberg. Fast forward 43 years to 2002 and a new film *The Pornographer*. With a title like that it doesn't need me to tell you that it is based in a shady, shocking world peopled by shady, shocking types. Yet *Sunday Times* film critic Cosmo Landesman was moved to remark, 'What is going on with the French? *The Pornographer* is a downbeat art-house movie, and not one character smokes!'

In reality the culture of smoking in the Western world has changed enormously and even the most passionate pro-smoker would be pushed to complain. Legislation now prohibits people who handle food from smoking or chewing tobacco so the age of finding ash in your restaurant dinner has been dispatched to history.

Smoking is also forbidden on just about all forms public transport, a rule that can be a strain for chain smokers. One scene in the comedy series *Absolutely Fabulous* cleverly demonstrates the plight of the smoker in our non-smoking society as Patsy, played by Joanna Lumley, removes her top after a transatlantic flight to reveal a back plastered in nicotine patches. But most people agree that smoke-free zones are a huge improvement – where there's no smoking, there are no dog-ends and the attendant fire risk, thus planes, trains, and boats have become safer, cleaner, more sanitary places.

In addition, many work places are now smoke free zones enabling office workers to breathe cleaner air and reducing the amount of germs flying around public building expelled during smokers' coughs.

02 WORLD

'Cigarette, coffee, make-up. I can't face the day without them.' Cindy Blackmore, 27, a secretary from Liverpool, England, sets out her priorities for the day. 'Sometimes I skip breakfast but I never miss that first fag – or the second one, for that matter. It's just my way of getting by.'

That's what addiction does for you: it shapes your outlook and changes what is important to you. Everyone has a schedule in which they prioritize the things that are paramount. Included in it may be parents, siblings, children, computers, clothes, cars, bikes, football, theatre and so forth.

Once you are addicted to something, you find it has wriggled its way into your affections and, before you know it, has taken over your life. Yes, it is important to see your parents, but the trip assumes greater appeal if they have spare cigarettes. True, a visit to your sister is a duty that's a pleasure but you do so less if she lives in a non-smoking house. You may look forward to playing a particular computer game – but you will embark on the adventure only after a cigarette, stopping throughout for fag breaks. There's an unmissable play on at the theatre but it becomes, well, missable if it means you have to skip on cigarettes while you are penned inside the auditorium.

At first cigarettes are not addictive. The dependency creeps up on you in a sinister fashion. People often accept their first cigarette out of curiosity, to discover the attraction its holds for millions worldwide. It is between two weeks and three months before cigarette addiction sets in.

Smoking soon sets a framework for the day. People smoke with a morning coffee – another addiction – or their first alcoholic drink of the day. Soon they cannot have one without the other and the ritual element of smoking – as important today as it was for the American Indians centuries ago – makes it as hard to quit the habit as the addiction to nicotine.

The sensory benefits of nicotine are difficult to resist. It stimulates instantaenously and as the heart races, causing blood to pump, the smoker is ready for action. Yet with chameleon-like skill it also relaxes people when they feel tense. Lighting up helps to concentrate the wandering minds of some, who claim they are less tired and less bored with a cigarette in their hand.

What happens is that nicotine sparks the electric circuitry of the brain. In doing so it sends neurotransmitters called dopamine between nerve cells, creating reward pathways. This the brain likes but it is not so keen when the dopamine disappears again. Repeated doses of nicotine ensure the maintenance of these happy feelings. Nicotine has been shown to have effects on brain dopamine systems similar to those of drugs such as heroin and cocaine.

There's dispute (of course) about whether smokers are truly addicted. 'The word addiction has become almost meaningless,' according to Simon Clark at Forest. He points out that these days the term 'addict' is applied to someone who eats a lot of chocolate, likes shopping, plays the lottery, often submits to cosmetic surgery, frequently surfs the Internet or pursues a host of other activities, innocuous or otherwise.

'We think it is counter production to teach people they are addicted. They immediately say, "I'm an addict, I'm a victim" and there is someone else to blame.

'When adults are perhaps smoking 100 cigarettes a day, the problem is a psychological one. That person has an addictive personality. If it wasn't cigarettes that was their weakness it would be something else like drink or gambling.

'If smokers actually wanted to give up they could. It takes a lot of will power, it is a very difficult habit to break, but 11 million people have given up smoking in the UK alone. That figure doesn't suggest it is an impossible feat to accomplish.'

His view gets support from Professor John Davis of the University of Strathclyde, who says, 'What I don't agree with is the idea that people who use nicotine become…helpless addicts who have no say in the choice of this activity, that the nicotine compels them to smoke. The evidence is simply not there. People give up smoking all the time.'

Addiction is all about habit and compulsion. *The Oxford Compact English Dictionary*'s definition of an addict is an enthusiastic devotee of a pastime. Put with nicotine, the word addict seems to bear a far more cataclysmic meaning and is only a hair's breadth away from the term abuse.

> 'I would argue that every man, whatever his race, whatever his rank, whatever his profession, whatever his work, is helped by smoking.' Sir Compton Mackenzie (1883-1972)

Dr Hans Eysenck (1916-97), the eminent German psychologist, disliked such terms being bandied about. He insisted that smoking was not an addiction 'because the term addiction really has no scientific meaning. It is used in so many different ways that it is almost impossible to attach any meaning to it. This idea is not really controversial, there have been several books on it recently with people making exactly the same point. You could call sex addictive, or reading in my case, or playing tennis, you can call anything addictive which a person does routinely and which he would be sorry to stop doing and which might have all sorts of repercussions on his mental and physical life.' Eysenck also remained sceptical about the link between lung cancer and smoking.

But the Royal College of Physicians has come up with a convincing argument to prove in the minds of many that nicotine addiction is alive and well and flourishing among smokers.

'The majority of smokers who develop cardiovascular disease are still smoking a year later.' (This happens even when they get quality care and support in the art of giving up smoking and when they know their health would improve by quitting.) 'One recent UK study assessed smoking cessation one year after patients were newly diagnosed with myocardial infarction or angina. Only 20 per cent of 169 patients smoking in the two weeks prior to diagnosis had managed to quit smoking a year later, despite support by trained nurses and an average of more than two quit attempts by these patients throughout the year.'

Even more worrying was the inability to quit displayed among one section of the seriously ill. 'Buerger's disease is a progressive inflammatory occlusive disease almost exclusive to smokers, which commonly requires surgical intervention including limb amputation. Prognosis for Buerger's disease is considerably improved by stopping smoking.

'One recent study followed a cohort of 69 such patients over the first ten years after diagnosis. All but one of the patients were smokers at the time of diagnosis and 84 per cent continued to smoke thereafter. Among those who continued to smoke, 65 per cent required amputation, almost twice the percentage of those who stopped smoking.'

Not all smokers are addicted, only most, says the Royal College of Physicians. 'It has been estimated that only about five per cent of smokers are able to smoke without becoming addicted.'

Cigarettes are today's preferred way of consuming tobacco but it wasn't always so. The first smokers used pipes made of clay or other basic materials. Sailors who saw Native Americans puffing away at pipes in the New World were responsible for spreading its practice around the so-called civilized world. Britain and Holland were centres of the clay pipe industry and everyone who smoked was comforted by the view, widely held, that they were doing themselves some good.

In the 1994 play *Tulip Futures* by John Constable, set in 17th-century Holland, there's a scene between the characters Dr Tulp and Willem-Jan which brilliantly reflects one commonly held medical view in Holland at that time.

(Dr Tulp offers Willem-Jan a clay pipe.)
WILLEM-JAN: Thanks. I don't.

DR TULP *(in mock horror)*: A Dutchman without a pipe, m'neer, is a spring bereft of flowers.

WILLEM-JAN: Makes me cough and wheeze.

DR TULP: Yes, some people have that reaction at first. Worth persevering. Tobacco stimulates the circulation of the blood, whilst sedating the brain. I've used it to cure worms and scurvy, rheum and ague, flux, pox. *(Puffs on his pipe, ruminating.)* Yes, I would go so far as to predict that Nicotiana will one day be recognized as a universal panacea.

WILLEM-JAN: I'll give it another try. *(Takes the other pipe, filling it with tobacco.)*

DR TULP: I used to prescribe it to my expectant mothers. Eases the labour and builds up the child's resistance. It has also proved remarkably effective against the plague. During the '35 epidemic, I always smoked on duty. *(Willem-Jan lights his pipe, coughing and wheezing. Dr Tulp laughs good-naturedly.)* Fumigates the lungs, you see... When I was dressing the corpses, you may be sure my pipe never left my mouth. *(Enter his wife, Griet, carrying a tray.)* The cadavers are extremely infectious, especially when the buboes burst.

GRIET: Klass! Please.

In an era when the bubonic plague was a frequent visitor to western Europe tobacco seemed a singular hope in a sea of despair. In 1636 Dutch doctor Isbrand van Diemerbroek believed he was only saved from the plague by smoking 'six or seven pipes of tobacco'.

The earliest pipes were hand made but from 1580 brass moulds were used to shape the clay. In the 18th-century the moulds were made of cast iron. The stem hole was formed when the clay was pierced by wire. After they were shaped the pipes were fired in kilns, often alongside items of pottery. In a rare find four pipe kilns dating from the late 17th century were discovered in Portsmouth, a naval centre in England. Advertisements in another port, Barnstaple in North Devon, appearing in the middle of the 19th century priced a 15" (38cm) fluted pipe at 1s 3d ($6^1/_2$p/10 ¢). A bigger, grander model cost 2s 9d (25 ¢). Evidence suggests that publicans gave away a basic pipe free with a pint of beer.

With every pipe produced there was an opportunity for artistic licence. Soon the bowls appeared in fancy design, including an eagle's claw clutching an egg or sculptures of famous people. A hunting dog clung to the stem of one pipe while the bowl of another was formed from a lady's leg, thigh uppermost. Pipes for upper-class men and women were made of silver. In 1850 the 'yard of clay' or 'Churchwarden' was introduced, literally a yard or metre in length. Although this was bordering on the absurd, the 'Churchwarden' did amply illustrate that pipe bowls had got bigger and bigger since first made in the 16th century, to accommodate ever larger amounts of (ever-cheaper) tobacco.

> 'Lastly (and this is, perhaps, the golden rule) no woman should marry a tee-totaller, or a man who does not smoke.'
> *Virginbus Puerisque* by Robert Louis Stevenson (1850–94)

Pipes made in England and Holland were shipped all over the world during the early years of the tobacco industry. Later, France became a centre of pipe production where the technique of clay tinting was perfected.

The arrival of cigarettes at the same time as the production of the briarwood pipe crippled the clay pipe industry and brought about its downfall. But, as a testament to its previous popularity, clay pipes remain one of the most common discoveries on archaeological excavations.

Even today pipes are associated with dependable, stoic, patriotic types. Pipe smoking used to be closely linked to the middle classes, as novelist EM Forster (1879–1970) observed in his *Notes On The English Character*.

'It is not that the Englishman can't feel – it is that he is afraid to feel. He has been taught at his public school that feeling is bad form. He must not express great joy or sorrow, or even open his mouth too wide when he talks – his pipe might fall out if he did.'

One of the best known names in the pipe world is that of Alfred Dunhill, who took over his father's London livery business in 1893 at the age of 21. It was an era of change, not least because of the growing popularity of the automobile. Dunhill was anxious about the prospects for the livery trade and was seeking to diversify. So he listened with interest to the complaints of motorists who found themselves unable to keep their pipes alight as they sped along in the new-fangled motorized contraptions.

In 1904 Dunhill patented the Windshield pipe with its raised front portion, designed to continue to smoulder in a rush of wind. Three years later Dunhill opened a pipe shop at 30 Duke Street in St James, London, and, later, a pipe factory next door. By 1916 Dunhill pipes, distinguished by a white spot, were selling for three times the amount of rival pipes.

Sir Compton MacKenzie, First World War veteran, intelligence office and author of *Whisky Galore*, was a keen pipe smoker. He estimated that he had smoked as much as a quarter of a million pipefuls of tobacco, producing a volume of smoke that 'might not disgrace Vesuvius when not in full eruption'. The penalties of smoking escaped him. 'My memory is crystal clear. My power of concentration is undiminished. My digestion is perfect. My heart is sound.' Indeed, he died just short of his 90th birthday.

> 'A cigarette that bears a lipstick's traces/ An airline ticket to romantic places/And still my heart has wings/These foolish things/Remind me of you. Holt Marvell, 'These Foolish Things', 1935

Snuff tried to edge pipe smoking into obscurity when it made inroads into British culture in the 17th century. However, its dominance lasted little more than a century although it endured for longer in Europe. Snuff is, of course, powdered tobacco, which can be inhaled or rubbed on the teeth and gums. During production tobacco is fermented and may even be suffused with the scent of herbs, spices and flowers.

When Charles II returned to the British throne in 1660 he brought with him the French predelection for snuff. Soon snuff was the last word in fashion among aristocrats. At first, each dose was hand grated from a block of dark tobacco. Snuff takers armed themselves with graters made of ivory and precious metals for the purpose. Snuff became more fashionable still with the advent of decorative snuff boxes, small enough to slip into a waistcoat pocket but nonetheless elaborate. Snuff box lids might feature miniature paintings, gems, cameos or family crests. Women as well as men took snuff and Queen Charlotte (1744-1818), wife of Britain's King George III, was foremost among them. Such was her liking for it she was known as 'snuffy Charlotte'.

Thomas Macaulay (1800-59) recalled the lofty position snuff assumed in society by describing its widespread use in coffee houses. 'If any clown,

Elderly American woman taking a pinch of snuff, c1855.

A GROUP OF SIOUX INDIANS.

A group of Sioux Indians, c1875, holding peace pipes. American Indians chewed, sniffed, and drank tobacco as well as smoking it in pipes. They probably also used it in medicine and ceremonially from the first century BC.

ignorant of the usages of the house, called for a pipe the sneers of the whole assembly and the short answers of the waiters soon convinced him that he had better go somewhere else.'

Snuff was inhaled and expelled in the next breath from a pinch held between forefinger and thumb, with the chief reward being a sneeze. A deep-seated, satisfying sneeze is always followed by a sense of well-being and perhaps for this reason snuff was used for medicinal purposes.

Although snuff was largely the reserve of the upper classes, the habit did catch on among poorer people who 'cut' their meagre supplies of tobacco with other substances, like coal dust.

Snuff fell from grace in Britain when it became associated with Roman Catholicism, at a time when the religious divide of the country was a vital issue. London doctor John Hill did much to cap the use of snuff when in 1761 he reported that it was the cause of cancers of the nose.

While pipe smoking or snuff were the preferred options for most Europeans, chewing tobacco – otherwise known as spit tobacco – was the people's choice in the United States, a habit they had borrowed from the American Indians. The pioneers of the Wild West could hardly stop to re-light their pipes every few minutes as they galloped across the plains. Nor could a rough, tough cowboy be seen to pepper the back of his hand with tobacco and delicately inhale during, say, a cattle round-up. Chewing tobacco was a far more convenient, portable habit.

Produced in different varieties, the most familiar of these were 'flat plug', made from bright tobacco and sometimes sweetened; 'navy', made from barley tobacco and flavoured with sweeteners or spices; 'twist', robust dark tobacco rolled into ropes; 'fine-cut', a more refined alternative or 'scrap', the by-products of cigar-making procedures.

Tobacco played a prominent part as the wild west was won. In a pen portrait of the Texas cowboy, the *Daily Commonwealth* of 15 August 1871 wrote, 'His diet is principally Navy plug and whisky, and the occupation of his heart is gambling.'

With the popularity of chewing tobacco came some gross personal habits that in retrospect make the stomach churn. It made the mouth fluids brown and sticky and the evacuation of this fluid, stored hamster-like in the cheeks, became a matter of urgency.

Soon spittoons – metal or earthenware pots for punters to spit into – had become a necessity. They were placed at strategic points around a saloon or pub to catch the flying phlegm. History holds no testimony from the poor souls whose job it was to clean the spittoon when it overflowed. Walking across the saloon inadequately furnished with spittoons must have been a treacherous business and lends a whole new meaning to the phrase 'slippery customer'.

The extent of the popularity of chewing tobacco is indicated in the 1860 census for Virginia and North Carolina. Of 348 tobacco factories listed in the census 335 concentrated wholly on producing chewing tobacco. Only six were concerned with marketing tobacco for smoking, produced primarily from the scraps of chewing tobacco.

The arrival of cheap, mass-produced cigarettes appeared to mark the end of an era for chewing tobacco and after the First World War its popularity plummeted.

However, a perception that it is less harmful than cigarettes inspired a recent revival in its fortunes in America. In 1993 low-nicotine, cherry-flavoured Skoal Long Cut was launched in the US, an attractive purchase for young people. Health agencies were forced to move quickly to address the growing popularity of smokeless tobacco.

> Research shows that 75 per cent of black smokers in America prefer menthol cigarettes compared with 20 per cent of white smokers. First-time teen smokers are also more likely to choose menthol.

The hookah, also known as the nargile or waterpipe, originated in India but became the people's choice for tobacco smoking in Turkey. Tremendous etiquette surrounded the smoking of the hookah. It consists of a mouthpiece, traditionally made of amber, attached to a smoking tube, a neck – perhaps brass – and a bowl filled with water. Hot charcoal is placed upon the tobacco plug. Dark tobacco from Iran was the preferred option and some users added fruit or scents to the water for flavour.

Diplomatic relations between the once-mighty Ottoman Empire and the rest of the world were forged or broken over a hookah. Initially an implement of high fashion, the hookah fell victim to the popularity of cigarettes although it is still smoked in selected salons.

One user explained its advantage over smokes. 'Cigarettes are for nervous people, competitive people, people on the run. When you smoke a nargile you have time to think. It teaches you patience and tolerance and gives you an appreciation of good company. Nargile smokers have a much more balanced approach to life than cigarette smokers.'

To this day, cigars remain conspicuous symbols of wealth and power. Fidel Castro, the president of Cuba, who gleefully baits his northerly neighbour the United States with a self-proclaimed Marxist-Leninist political programme, is renowned for his cigar smoking. It is strange how this capitalist emblem became indelibly associated with Communist Castro. Even more galling for the capitalists of the 'better dead than red' brigade who held sway in the '60s was the fact that they were finding Havanas rather difficult to obtain while the Commies were enjoying a plethora. This is because sanctions issued by the US meant that, in most circumstances, importation of Cuban cigars into America was prohibited. Similar rules are still in place today, making the smuggling of Cuban cigars a profitable business. Cigar smoking has remained a popular pastime even when a 5" (12.5cm) cigar as thick as your thumb produces 30 times as much carbon monoxide as a cigarette.

Lord Byron was an advocate of using tobacco in general and cigars in particular, as this extract from one of his poems demonstrates:

> 'Sublime tobacco! Which from East to west
> Cheers the Tar's labor or the sultan's rest...
> Divine in Hookahs, glorious in a pipe
> When tipped with amber, mellow, rich and ripe;
> Like other charmers, wooing the caress,
> More dazzling when daring in full dress;
> Yet thy true lovers more admire by far
> They make beauties – give me a cigar.'

Cigars were handmade and the Cigar Makers' International Union demanded that workers served a three-year apprenticeship in the art. Only after the

1850s were moulds used in cigar manufacture, radically improving the rate at which they were produced.

Otto von Bismarck (1815–98), Prussia's Iron Chancellor, enjoyed a cigar. He insisted, '[It] acts as a mild sedative without in any way impairing our mental faculties. [It] is a sort of diversion, as the blue smoke curls upward the eye involuntarily follows it, the effect is soothing, one feels better tempered.'

'Poker Alice' Tubbs (1851–1930), the British-born card sharp who haunted boom towns of the Wild West, was a copious cigar smoker. Despite the dangers to her health from the smoke, six-shooters and an uncertain career, she survived until she was 79.

Ally Sloper, the hero of the world's first regular comic strip, which appeared between 1884 and 1920 in a British weekly paper, was depicted with a cigar in his hand. Ally and his cigars inhabited an era where the wellborn still wore top hats and lived in opulence.

The richly appointed smoking room on the ill-fated *Titanic* was out-of-bounds for women and was inhabited by some of the first-class male passengers enjoying a cigar at the moment the ship collided with an iceberg. But the *Titanic*, just like the cloistered aristocracy of the time, was nearing the end of a hallowed existence. By the end of the First World War the splendid isolation of the British upper classes had largely disappeared. With it went the vogue for cigar smoking, to be replaced largely with cigarettes. Cigar smoking continued but was detached from class distinction. Paraphernalia from this golden age of cigar smoking, including cigar bands and cigar silks – both used in the presentation of an expensive brand – are still bought and sold as collectibles today.

Sir Winston Churchill (1874–1965) was of course known for liking cigars. His antagonism towards Labour politician Sir Stafford Cripps (1889–1952) was only tempered by a mutual enjoyment of cigars. When he heard that Cripps had given up smoking he expressed his regret, saying that the cigar was Cripps's last contact with humanity. Other cigar smokers of note include Karl Marx, Groucho Marx, James Cagney, Somerset Maugham, PG Wodehouse, George Sand, and Eleanor Roosevelt.

Today cigars are sometimes used as a none-too-subtle phallic symbol. Ballet dancer Sylvie Guillem takes sensual, needy puffs from an outsized cigar with her legs splayed and her bosom heaving during her portrayal as a sex-crazed Carmen in a Royal Ballet production, choreographed by Mats Ek. In the original story of *Carmen*, written in 1845 by Prosper Merimee, the title character is a cigarette girl in an Andalusian factory. Former US President Bill Clinton, with his liking for cigars and his presumed weakness for sexual liaisons, has done much to further the cigar's image as a penis replacement.

Cigars have numerous identities. For example, a corona is a straight cigar measuring some $5^1/_2$" (14cm), with a rounded end that goes in the mouth. The coronas then descend in order of size as follows: petit corona, tres petit corona and half a corona, coming in at about $3^3/_4$" (9.5cm) in length. Similar in shape to the corona but slightly longer is the Lonsdale. The Ideales is a thin, torpedo cigar measuring some $6^1/_2$" (16.5cm). Bouquet and Londres cigars are similarly thin but shorter. One of the most popular and accessible of the cigar family is the panatela, which is slim, about 5" (12.7cm) long and is sometimes distinguished by being pinched at the mouth end. Once it had a finished top that had to be severed before smoking but this is not often the case nowadays. A cheroot is usually beefier than a panatela, and shorter. In Britain a small cigar open at both ends is called a whiff.

> 'Though smokers generally know they face increased risks and are warned to that effect, they judge the magnitude and diversity of these risks to be lower and less well established than they actually are.' Royal College of Physicians

Cigars come in different colours. These are claro (CCC), the lightest, going through colourado-claro (CC), colourado (C), colourado-maduro (CM) and maduro (M), the darkest. The colour coding refers less to the wrap on the cigar and more to the tobacco inside. There's nothing slapdash about cigars. Sometimes cigar tobacco is stored for four years or more before being turned into a smoke. The challenge is to find the most pleasing aroma and appealing taste in an ever-more competitive market.

Modern cigars are generally sold in a protective cellophane wrapper. This is to help maintain temperature and humidity. More expensive brands favour the aluminium tube.

Cigarettes too have different tastes and strengths. Three main types of tobacco predominate: Virginia (or flue cured), Burley, and Oriental. In Britain the taste is for Virginia tobacco, just as it was when tobacco was first cultivated in America. Meanwhile, American smokers are partial to blends of Virginian, Burley, and Oriental tobaccos. Brazil, America, and Zimbabwe are among the countries that grow flue-cured tobacco while Malawi is a producer of Burley.

Cigarette papers have a science all to themselves. It is the paper that's responsible for how quickly a cigarette burns and the thickness of smoke it produces. The paper is designed to burn when the smoker takes a drag but to slow to a smoulder when it is in hand. Papers are drenched in chemicals to help achieve this perfect burn.

Many of today's cigarettes bear filter tips, which have become popularly perceived as a health aid since the early 1950s. Made from a fibre called cellulose, its purpose is apparently to reduce the amount of smoke that reaches the lungs. (An early filter tip made with asbestos has long since disappeared.) When smokers were permitted to light up in cinemas, many were left coughing and spluttering in an acrid cloud after lighting the filter tip in error in the darkness.

At some point along the length of a cigarette filter you can usually find ventilation holes designed to reduce the delivery of tar, nicotine and carbon monoxide to the smoker. And that's exactly what happens when the cigarettes are tested by machine. In reality, these holes are often covered by lips or fingers, and so the tar and nicotine measurements of the cigarette are raised. Contrary to one urban legend circulating in the recent past, tobacco companies do not spike cigarettes with nicotine to keep the smoker smoking. Nicotine occurs naturally in tobacco so no one need go to the trouble of introducing it. It is true that tobacco is modified in cigarette production with additives, such as flavouring. Usually added to give a characteristic brand taste, to give the blend uniformity or to preserve freshness, these additives could well assist with the delivery of nicotine.

One of the most commonly used flavourings is menthol, which is supposed to give cigarettes a smoother taste. Some experts are now concerned that the smokers of menthol cigarettes develop the habit of taking deeper drags, introducing more nicotine to their systems and tar to their lungs.

'For decades we took the approach that tobacco products were so deadly, the ingredients were basically a side issue,' says Jack Henningfield of Johns Hopkins University. 'We're recognizing ingredients can make a lot of difference.'

As ever, in the field of cigarettes, smoking, and tobacco, the debate about whether or not these additives have any physiological effects is by no means settled.

Cigarette smoke has been extensively studied and is known to contain thousands of different elements. One informed estimate says that there are about 4,000 constituents formed when a cigarette is alight, most in minute quantities.

As cigarettes took over in popularity from cigars, cigarette cases and other accessories associated with cigarette smoking became highly fashionable. Those created in Peter Carl Fabergé's workshops in Tsarist Russia were probably the finest. He and his master craftsmen used precious metals, including silver and gold, wood, nephrite, jade and other semi-precious stones to embellish these cases. Others were enamelled or engraved. Many were studded with gems.

'Road accidents, suicide, murder, AIDS and drugs and solvents all kill. Smoking kills five times more people before their time thann all these other causes of death put together. Smoking is the biggest single cause of preventable disease and premature death in this country.' 'Smoking And Your Child', issued by Britain's Department of Health

Britain's King Edward VII himself owned an exquisite red-gold case covered in blue enamel, bearing a snake picked out in rose diamonds, given to him by his friend Mrs Alice Keppel.

In 1914 Fabergé made a silver cigarette case bearing a sunburst pattern with a gold monogram for Grand Duke Michael Michaelovitch, whose days of influence and privilege in Russia were by now numbered. There were matchboxes, too, and table lighters. These were highly desirable objects among Europe's élite. Smoking cigarettes gave them a great excuse to spend a fortune on beautiful accessories.

Cigarettes have played a role in the dark side of history, too. Notorious as an implement of torture, cigarettes have been, and still are, wielded against prisoners of war, victims of interrogation and children. But they can also be the final taste of life for a condemned man, whose last request is often for a cigarette. Caryl Chessman, convicted as the Red Light Bandit of Hollywood in 1948, became a legal expert, writer, and reformed character during his years on death row. But his change of heart did not extend to smoking. Before

In 1990 Rev Calvin Butts, the pastor of Harlem's Abyssinian Baptist Church, began a campaign of whitewashing inner-city billboards that showed advertisements for tobacco or alcohol.

he was led to the gas chamber on 2 May 1960 he smoked a final cigarette before his lungs were ravaged by far more noxious gases. So ingrained in the public imagination is the idea of the 'last smoke' that there was outcry recently when a condemned man in America was denied his last request for a cigarette.

Despite being a symbol of freedom for many, cigarette's connection to disease and death is always present. Every cigarette package carries some kind of warning. Among the best-known are 'smoking kills', 'smoking while pregnant can harm your baby' and 'blah, blah, blah'.

If you started dozing off for a bit there, you are not alone. It seems that the government health warnings are a major turn-off for smokers and potential smokers. Start spouting the science and we just glaze over.

In Canada, where cigarettes are sold in packs of 25, new steps have been taken to conquer the switch-off syndrome. There, cigarette packets must by law bear full-colour pictures detailing the effects of smoking alongside some hard-hitting slogans. Furthermore, these graphic warnings must cover more than half the pack and are reinforced by written warnings in English and French on the inside of the pack. Little attempt has been made to spare the finer feelings of the smoker who might choke on his smoke as he takes a forced reality-check on just what the smoke is doing to his insides. Manufacturers have a choice of 16 warnings, a few of which are outlined here.

German Chancellor Adolf Hitler (1889–45), who launched the first anti-smoking campaign in the world. Magazines and newspapers were filled with warnings of the dangers of cigarettes. One magazine asked, 'Brother national socialist, do you know that our Führer is against smoking and thinks that every German is responsible to the whole people for all his deeds and emissions and does not have the right to damage his body with drugs?'

Winston Churchill (1874–1965), British statesman and Prime Minister for two terms (1940–45 and 1951–55). Churchill is one of several 20th-century icons – including Al Capone, Bob Dylan, Che Guevara, Humphrey Bogart, and Noël Coward – whose image is closely associated with smoking.

Wounded US soldiers of the 3rd Battery, 16th Infantry Regiment, 1st US Infantry Division, leaning against chalk cliffs while eating and smoking after storming Omaha Beach in Collville-Sur-Mer, Normandy, France, during World War II. Cigarettes were an essential provision for many soldiers.

One warning shows a photo of a disgustingly diseased mouth, complete with yellow teeth and receding, bloodied gums, accompanied by the phrase 'cigarettes cause mouth diseases'. Another picture of a wilting cigarette endorses the message 'Tobacco use can make you impotent'. It is further embellished with the words 'cigarettes may cause sexual impotence due to decreased blood flow to the penis'.

A picture of a serene, sleeping baby is tagged with the blunt words 'Tobacco smoke hurts babies'. Two other slogans are 'each year the equivalent of a small city dies from tobacco use' and 'where there's smoke there's hydrogen cyanide'.

But the most controversial remain: 'cigarettes are a heart breaker' accompanied by the picture of a damaged heart and 'cigarettes cause lung cancer' illustrated by a body on a ventilator.

For the Canadian government these hard-hitting warnings are all about providing information 'in a meaningful way'.

Clive Bates, the director of ASH, is unequivocal in his support of the scheme. 'If these warnings prompt people to stop and think again, then they will save thousands of lives in the long term. It's all about cutting through the denial and getting smokers to confront the desperate reality of cancer, heart disease and emphysema head on.

'The pictures grab you at a gut level and communicate in the same way as advertising. This is proper risk communication whereas the current weedy and virtually invisible warnings almost suggest that there isn't that much to worry about.'

But other people believe that shock tactics like these ultimately raise the threshold of tolerance among smokers, inuring them to the anti-smoking rhetoric.

The same debate is mirrored in the drugs scene. In 2002 the heartbroken parents of a British heroin addict agreed for shocking pictures of her dead body to be used in an educational video. She was found on her knees with a syringe still clutched in her hand.

'Bravo!' shouted one side who believed the horrifying photos would make people think twice before taking up drugs. 'Not so,' retorted the other, citing that it obliquely glamorized the drug in the eyes of young people.

The truth is probably somewhere in the middle. The explicit warnings on cigarette packets and in videos will shape the views of some young people, especially if they have yet to embark on a life with fags or drugs. But there is a group of hardline hedonists who will not be deterred no matter how many graphic images are presented to them.

Further changes to the appearance of a cigarette packet in the 21st century are imminent after the 'safer' cigarette was revealed as a sham.

For years smokers convinced themselves they were doing themselves good – or at least, less harm – if they indulged in 'reduced' cigarettes. The descriptions for such products included 'lite', 'mild', 'low tar' or 'low nicotine'. Sometimes the marketing was directed specifically at women.

Recently tobacco companies have admitted that 'lite' brands are no less harmful to health than full strength. Indeed, sometimes these brands are even more toxic than their counterparts. The hidden danger is that they might be more unsatisfactory to smokers who then inhale more deeply and light up more often.

Brazil was the first country in the world to ban cigarettes described as 'lite'. Canada followed suit and Israel also took action under their 1981 Consumer Protection Law. The European parliament has pressed its members to bar 'lite' brands by the year 2003.

In America during 2002 a jury in Oregon ruled that the tobacco company Philip Morris must pay $150 million to the family of a woman who died of lung cancer. The jury found that the company falsely represented low tar cigarettes as healthier. Further lawsuits following the same vein are in the pipeline.

'Lite' cigarettes occupy the biggest portion of the American market. Many smokers switched to light brands on the advice of former US Surgeon General Julius Richmond in 1981 when it was believed the associated health risks were lower. His recommendation was aimed at those people who found themselves unable to quit and the advice has long been dropped. One smoker from Florida explained his argument with the cigarette manufacturers. 'The word "light" itself meant to me that it would probably be better for you. Why should a company make a profit on something they lied to the people about?'

However, many tobacco companies still use the term light to describe cigarettes with less than 15 milligrams of tar. It is not, they insist, and never was meant to be an indication of safety.

Although there are a significant number of smokers in society, their right to light up where and when they feel the need have been severely eroded of late. In Tamil Nadu, India, anyone who smokes or spits in public places faces a fine and may be jailed for three months for repeat offences. Cigarette and tobacco advertising on the streets is also banned.

In New York smoking is banned in all restaurants with more than 35 seats and in almost all buildings open to the public. But it is California that is the beacon of anti-smoking legislation in America. From 1998 the state has boasted some trail-blazing new laws. Light up inside a restaurant, pub or club and you find yourself on the wrong side of the law. The measures are tough but have ridden out opposition to become largely popular among young people.

Restaurant owners across the globe have expressed concern that

> One of the earliest chain smokers was Napoleon III (1808–73), who was known for watching his troops on the battle-fields of Europe while drawing deeply on a cigarette for courage.

smoking restrictions would mean loss of trade. In fact, there's some evidence that new business is acquired from people who would otherwise steer clear of smoky environments. That view is endorsed by 16-year-old Tahni Bolshaw: 'Restaurants should all be "no smoking". Many are half smoking half not and the smoke just whiffs across. I used to work as a waitress and customers would just blow the smoke in your face. It was disgusting.'

A survey carried out by the California Department of Health Services in August 1998 revealed that 65 per cent of bar customers approved of the smoke-free law. The number had risen from 59 per cent in a similar survey carried out six months previously. An astonishing 87 per cent of bar patrons said they would go out for a drink more often following the law that made smoking in public places illegal, rather than less.

The anti-smoking message is not getting through everywhere in the Western world. British-born Sabra Kemner lives in Holland where she notices a reluctance to embrace a smoke-free environment.

'When I first came to live in the Netherlands, I became immediately aware of a difference in attitude towards smoking compared with the UK. Eleven years later and nothing seems to have changed.

'A lot more people seem to smoke in general and especially in public places where smoky air can frequently be quite overwhelming and far worse than I was used to. A lot of people also seem to roll their own cigarettes with so-call "shag", which leaves a particularly strong after-smell. If you happen to spend a few hours in a bar then your clothes will reek so badly that you can smell them even when they are contained in a closed washing basket!

'People don't think twice about lighting up in a restaurant and smoking and non-smoking areas only seem to occur in institutions of non-Dutch origins such as McDonald's.

'People do not in general ask if you mind them smoking when they visit your house – or they might say, "You don't mind me smoking, do you?" in a way that means, "I'm going to smoke here whatever."

'In general there seems to be a much more nonchalant attitude towards smoking and, in fact, it almost seems an acceptable habit. While the health risks are not hidden, the Dutch seem busy with staying fit in other ways, such as jogging on a Sunday morning or cycling, taking long walks and so forth. They still seem to live long lives.

'Perhaps another significant factor is that cigarettes are quite cheap here and around half the retail price of the UK. Smoking is also perhaps a part of the culture here with a lot of people using so called Coffee Shops to hang out in and smoke tobacco or dope where it is allowed.'

In fact, there have been changes but they have been slow coming about by comparison to Britain and America.

Dutch cinemas are non-smoking now and there are 'no-smoking' carriages in trains. A 47-year-old family man who works at the Dutch airline KLM has also noticed changes creeping in to the attitude towards smoking. 'No one lights up in meetings anymore like they used to and they now have designated smoking areas for people who need to have a cigarette. People seem more aware of how smoking affects non-smokers than ever before.'

These small concessions sometimes leave Kemner frustrated. 'As a non-smoker I feel quite strongly that I have to suffer from other people's smoke. Smokers do not have the sense of smell of us non-smokers and do not realize what they are putting us through. A strong smell of smoke makes me feel quite nauseous and I resent that and the unapologetic attitude of smokers who make out that non-smokers are making a fuss over nothing.'

However, one 16-year-old Dutch girl typifies the national approach to smoking. 'I suppose I started smoking because I wanted to belong and all my mates smoked. I smoke a packet a day and don't worry about the cost.

'I don't intend to give up right now. My parents both smoked though my father had to give up for health reasons. They never tried to stop me as that would have been hypocritical.'

In 1902 Topsy the elephant killed her keeper, JF Blount, at Coney Island when he tried to feed her a lighted cigarette. She scooped him up in her trunk and hurled him to the ground. On 5 January 1903, 1,500 people gathered at Coney Island to watch Topsy's electrocution.

In Beijing those who smoke in public are fined. In London the issue of smoking in public places is under scrutiny. Most smaller communities are still reluctant to impose a complete ban on smoking. Recently the Canadian town of Stellarton refrained from becoming fume-free, partly because the smokeless zone would have incorporated premises belonging to the Royal Canadian Legion. Mayor Art Fitt said, 'A legion to these veterans is their home. These are fellows who fought overseas. Are we going to tell them not to light up a cigarette?'

The 'smoke-free' legislation is steered by a general belief that it is impossible to achieve an acceptable level of air cleanliness when smokers and non-smokers are in the same vicinity. One Canadian researcher said that only ventilation powered like a gale force wind could bring about the necessary air-exchange rate.

Needless to say, not everyone agrees. One restaurateur Antony Worrall Thompson, a patron of Forest, said, 'I believe that you can accommodate both smokers and non-smokers in public places by having genuinely smoke free areas. With proper ventilation and partitioning this can be achieved, although it must be understood that it can be a long and expensive process for proprietors. In the meantime we must defend freedom of choice. Legislation is not an option. Britain must not become a nanny state.'

For many years parents have curled up in angst when they discover offspring smoking cannabis. Surely this is the first step on the slippery path that will lead to hard drugs? Well, no, not necessarily. Cannabis has been carrying the can for the cigarette which, doctors insist, is the real entry drug, There are few hard drug users who haven't smoked at some time in their lives.

The question of how to stop young people smoking has been debated at length but never satisfactorily resolved.

'I insisted on having a puff when I was three years old,' says Erika Willson. 'My dad let me and I felt really, really sick. I never wanted to try it again.'

It was a technique that worked in this case, but effectiveness is not guaranteed. Another parental response brought about a different outcome, as Teresa Tucker explains: 'The first time I had a cigarette was when I was 11, with my friend Tracey. We knew where the sixth-formers hid their cigarettes when they didn't want to take them home – in the thick ivy on the wall where they got off the school bus – so we decided to pinch one and have a go. It was absolutely horrible.

'But my brother told my dad and he hit me with a wooden spoon. After that I swore I wouldn't give up and I didn't until I started trying for a family. That was more than ten years later.

'A friend of mine was made to sit down by his mother and smoke a whole packet of cigarettes in front of her. He went a funny shade of green, was as sick as a pig, and never smoked again. My friend Tracey is still smoking now.

'If I found my children smoking I wouldn't do what my dad did. I think they are going to try it whether you stop them or not. I may say here and now that I am not going to hit the roof but I probably will. But they are going to experiment and you can only warn them of the dangers and the addiction.'

At 22, actor Oli Couzens is desperate to stop smoking. 'When I started smoking at 14 people said to me, "It is the worst thing you can do." You won't be able to stop once you've started. I took no notice, I thought I would stop before I became addicted.

'Now I hear myself saying the same thing to kids, although I always swore to myself I wouldn't. I tell them, "Don't smoke, it is lethal." They look at me as if to say, "Yeah, right."

Oli was an underage smoker despite the fact his mother, a nurse, was ferocious in her opposition. 'My friends and I used to smoke in the middle of some holly bushes or in a little tin chicken shed at the bottom of the churchyard.

'When my mum confronted us one day my friend ran into the toilet to eat some toothpaste to mask the smell. There was none there so he took a bite out of the soap instead. Another time a friend stuffed a lit cigarette into his trouser pocket when my mum passed him in the street. Unfortunately for him, she stopped to talk to him. There was a hole scorched in his trousers and a burn mark on his leg before she moved on.'

> 'The humble cigarette is responsible for a dozen times more deaths in the UK in the past 40 years than British casualties from World War II – over five million. This is not a cold statistic but a human tragedy.' Sir George Alberti, Royal College of Physicians

It seems the degree to which children accept smoking – through seeing their parents do it, by watching screen idols indulge or being with best friends who are smokers – determines whether or not they will take it up. Trivial though it may seem, there's troubling evidence that children who buy imitation candy cigarettes are nearly four times more likely to sample the real thing.

Simon Clark, of Forest, contributes genetic evidence to the debate: 'According to two studies published in the *American Psychological Journal*, researchers found that people carrying a particular version of the dopamine transporter gene are less likely to start smoking before the age of 16 and more likely to be able to stop smoking if they start.'

So whether you are a smoker or a non-smoker could be determined by how you're made.

It is undoubtedly harder for smokers to prevent their children from smoking. Research has found that the offspring of smokers are almost twice as likely to smoke as children of non-smokers. Anyone who smokes but wants to stop their children from taking up the habit must communicate with their children on the issue. This is especially important as the child of a smoker is less likely to be detected because his or her parents cannot distinguish the smell of cigarette smoke on their clothes.

The best method of tackling the issue with your children is to ask them how they feel about smoking: follow it up with forthright, honest comments about your worries for them. Try to explain why you smoke and examine the nature of addiction. Avoid smoking rituals in front of them so they don't begin to associate a cigarette with a stressful situation, a certain television programme, the aftermath of a meal and so forth. Consider their comments carefully and make concessions on issues such as having a smoke-free home.

Research shows that parental disapproval plays its part as a deterrent whether or not parents are smokers. Anyone who discovers their children smoking is advised not to overreact. By talking through the situation it may be possible to establish why the child feels the need to smoke, how much they smoke and where they are getting the money. Then parents must walk a fine line between encouraging the smoker to quit and being seen as interfering or nagging.

Cigarette smoking has had extraordinary repercussions for Native Americans and Canadians. Before the arrival of Europeans there was no perceived problem with tobacco use. It was an important part of religious ceremony but was never used for leisure or pleasure.

'With the advent of cigarettes and particularly the distribution method of the cigarette vending machine, smoking has become an epidemic in people of the Cree Nation,' says Dr Bill Jacobs, Assistant Professor in Addiction Medicine at the University of Florida. 'They have a tremendous amount of guilt and shame – more than the average North American – because, whereas for us tobacco is not a religious object, it is for them and its flagrant use is almost blasphemy.'

Jacobs is now designing cessation programmes for Canadian First Nation people, which includes trained counsellors and an on-line 'virtual' treatment centre.

03 HISTORY

Christopher Columbus, Sir Francis Drake, and Sir Walter Raleigh have all been credited with bringing back the smoking habit from the New World and initiating a Western dependency on the weed.

Whoever takes the praise – or blame – they were to a man inspired by the activities of American Indians who chewed, sniffed and drank tobacco as well as smoking it in pipes.

The early history of tobacco use is largely guesswork. American Indians probably used it in medicine and ceremonially from the first century BC. Although archaeological evidence is sparse it is thought that the Mayans were smoking tobacco from about AD 500 as there are depictions of smokers on Guatemalan pottery dating between the 7th and 11th centuries AD.

Harper's *Encyclopaedia Of Mystical And Paranormal Experience* is unequivocal about the sacred importance of tobacco to the American Indians: 'Tobacco is believed to be endowed with supernatural powers to heal, hurt, bring luck, cause ill fortune and promote affection between husband and wife. It is smoked, snuffed, eaten, mixed in drinks and fermented [in] concoctions and burned as incense for rituals of harvest, war, puberty, death, initiation, purification, visions, communication with the spirits and gods and as part of pledges and oaths.'

When Indians died, tobacco and pipes were laid in their graves. Religiously important, yes, but Indians never puffed for the pleasure of it.

One mythological story says tobacco was a gift from the Great Spirit, to be used as a channel into a supernatural world. It is likely the Indians were mixing other types of leaf with the tobacco to achieve this 'other-worldliness', in pipes with stems made of hollow reeds, although the nicotine would have been stronger as present-day tobacco production methods reduce the content levels.

And, according to legend, the first pipe given to the earth by the Great Spirit had symbolic importance. Its bowl, carved in the likeness of a buffalo calf, represented the Earth and the four-legged creatures upon it. The stem symbolized all that grows on earth while the decorative eagle feathers represented the birds. In smoking all were united in a call to the Great Spirit.

When tobacco was alight the smoke, like breath, was thought to carry messages and prayers to the spirits. As a medicine it was blown over the affected body part of the patient by a medicine man as well as being smoked by the sick. The Aztecs believed tobacco to be sacred and thought that the body of their chief goddess Cihuacoahuati was composed of it. By the time the Europeans arrived tobacco was being traded between tribes and there were an estimated 600 words to describe it in their languages.

As every good student knows, Christopher Columbus (c1451–1506) discovered the New World and the tobacco plant growing there. It seems certain that tobacco leaves and seeds were brought back to Europe after his 1492 foray, having been given to Columbus as gifts by Arawak Indians in the West Indies. However, there is a delightful story that described how mystified Spanish sailors tossed the goods overboard into the sea, believing them to be useless.

History claims that sailor Rodrigo de Jerez, a companion of Columbus, was the first white man to start regularly smoking tobacco. He was allegedly reported to the Inquisition for his habit by someone who believed he was satanically possessed. His release occurred only after smoking became widespread in Spain.

An account of American Indians munching on tobacco leaves by Amerigo Vespucci (1451–1512), the man who gave his name to the Americas, appears in the 1507 book *Cosmographiae* by German cartographer Martin Waldesmuller.

Thanks to Columbus and those like Vespucci who followed in his wake, European cultivation of tobacco began as early as 1531 in Santo Domingo, now the capital of the Dominican Republic, where it soon became recognized as an efficient commercial crop. By 1580 it was growing in Cuba and from 1600 it was cultivated in Brazil.

When Jean Nicot de Villemain sent seeds to France from his ambassador's posting in Portugal in 1556 he gave his name to nicotine. At the time tobacco was available on the Iberian peninsula – it was even being grown in Portugal - but remained unknown in the rest of Europe.

Nicot studied the medicinal benefits of tobacco and, like other doctors in Spain and Portugal, was enthusiastic about its curative qualities. It quickly became an accepted remedy for toothache, worms, bad breath, lockjaw and cancer. A year later, *De Herbe Panacea*, featuring tobacco, was in publication. Other books enlightened Europeans about the use of tobacco among South American Indians. The Spanish Jesuit missionary Jose de Acosta included native tobacco consumption in his epic *De Natura Novi Orbis Libri Duo* in 1588 after he visited Peru. A year later came the work *Historia Natural Y Moral De Las Indias* which became required reading across Europe.

From Portugal tobacco use spread to Italy, India, Japan, Africa, and Arabia. Soon it was knocking at the door of that other emerging nation, Britain.

Adventurer Sir Francis Drake (c1540-96) took to the high seas more than 50 years after the death of Columbus, forming friendly relations with the Miwok Indians on America's Pacific Coast where he most likely developed a taste for tobacco.

Sir Walter Raleigh (c1554-1618) is the man behind the first organized English colony in North America at Roanoke, which ended in disaster. However, he is better remembered for persuading his patron Queen Elizabeth I to sample the delights of tobacco. Her teeth already black, she would have remained ignorant of one of its dental drawbacks. She was, by all accounts, mightily intrigued at his demonstration of tobacco usage and particularly in the way he measured the weight of tobacco smoke, which involved weighing the unsmoked weed then the ashes. By subtracting the second figure from the first he deduced the smoke's weight. Until Raleigh's time tobacco, also known as sotweed, was primarily used for medicine. During and after Raleigh's life it became a sociable pursuit.

The response to Raleigh's smoking was not always helpful. It is said his gardener tipped a bucket of water over his head, assuming him to be on fire after seeing clouds of smoke rising from his seated body.

Another Englishman, Sir John Hawkins (1532-95), is also believed to

Advertisement from 1945. Manufacturers have long promoted cigarettes as items of glamour and high fashion. Hollywood stars of the '30s, '40s, '50s, and '60s quite literally smouldered as they contemplated relations with an amour and the cigarette became a ready metaphor for sex.

American actor Steve McQueen (1930–80) during a break in production on the set of director Norman Jewison's film *The Thomas Crown Affair*.

Portrait of German actress Marlene Dietrich (1901–92). When Dietrich paraded through Rome in a jeep shortly after the city fell to the Allies, she was given an uproarious reception. 'It was like an Easter Parade – the boys threw cigarettes and chocolate,' she recalled later.

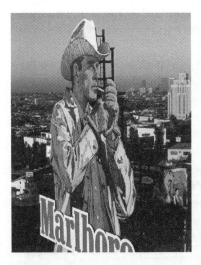

The Marlboro man epitomised the pulling power of advertising. Devised by Philip Morris, the Marlboro man was a physical Adonis who bore just the right amount of stubble, casual yet chic and rugged yet wise. He was the cowboy that every adolescent dreamed of being. He was the free spirit that every girl wanted to tame.

With a long cigarette holder, Princess Margaret Rose, younger daughter of King George VI and sister of Queen Elizabeth II, talks with actor Simon Callow and Emma Piper at the *Evening Standard* Drama Awards.

have introduced tobacco to British society. A relation of Drake's, he was a slave trader and ardent Protestant who played a significant part in driving the Catholic Spanish Armada into defeat in 1588. He is thought to have brought tobacco back from the Spanish West Indies during one of his early slave trading missions.

After pioneering nations like Portugal and Britain adopted the smoking habit it spread across central Europe, helped along by the soldiers of the 30 Years War (1618–48) who took it with them as they marched from battlefield to miserable battlefield in the heart of the continent.

Tobacco was by no means a universal hit. As its arrival post-dated both the Bible and the Koran, the written authorities of the time, rulers had no precedent to fall back upon and had to respond to this new habit by instinct. Tobacco's most famous opponent was King James I who, alerted to the expanding use of tobacco by physicians, was outraged that it was being used by people without prescription. James outlined his objections to it in an edict called *A Counterblaste To Tobacco* in 1604: 'Smoking is a custom loathsome to the eye, hateful to the nose, harmful to the brain, dangerous to the lungs, and in the black, stinking fume thereof nearest resembling the horrible Stygian smoke of the pit that is bottomless.'

James suspected that tobacco was linked to witchcraft, another pressing matter of state at the time. It must have been a tremendous shock for him to discover that, even after his opinions were made public, people up and down the kingdom were still smoking, chimney-like. For here was a man who considered himself invested with divine rights. As he explained to the English parliament, 'The state of monarchy is the supremest thing upon earth; for kings are not only God's lieutenants and sit upon a throne, but even by God himself they are called gods.'

The words of God's lieutenant were not enough to make people give up tobacco. After all, James was something of a laughing stock among the British people, most of whom were Protestant, while he was Catholic, and he was even branded by the French king as 'the wisest fool in Christendom'.

It was King James who saw to it that Sir Walter Raleigh was executed at the Tower of London in 1618 on a trumped-up charge of treason. Upon the adventurer's tobacco box, kept beside him for long years in the Tower, was the Latin inscription translated as 'It was my comfort in those miserable times.' Perhaps James' disposition towards Raleigh was coloured by his importation of tobacco or maybe his attitude to tobacco was as a result of an enmity towards the seafarer. At any rate, James went on to make the best of a bad job by burdening tobacco with extraordinary levels of tax.

The first Romanov tsar in Russia, Michael Feodorovich (1596-45), held similar sentiments to James I but exhibited his disapproval more forcefully. Those found guilty of smoking would have their lips slit or were flogged with that pernicious Russian whip, the knout. A few were castrated, although how this punishment fitted the crime no one knows. The lucky ones were merely exiled to Siberia.

In the Ottoman Empire thousands of hapless smokers were put to death in the early years of the 17th century upon the orders of a rabidly anti-smoking ruler, colloquially known as Murad the Cruel (1612-40). He banned smoking and shut down wine shops and coffee houses where the activity might take place. Legend holds that he roamed the streets of his kingdom in disguise asking for a cigarette then instantly pulling his sword and running through anyone who obliged him. Having caught a palace gardener and his wife smoking. Murad had their legs amputated and put them on public view as they bled to death. A smoker he wasn't but Murad was certainly possessed of an addictive and obsessive personality, and a dependence on drink brought about his early death.

The consumption of tobacco soon became a matter of papal concern. The Popes Urban VII (1521-90) and Innocent IX (1519-91) issued bulls excommunicating anyone who used snuff in church. Both popes held office

> 'Our lives as patients of chronic illnesses caused by smoking are filled with constant compromises and a sense of mourning for our bodies and what we have lost. We fight depression, exhaustion and a conscious knowledge that we are afflicted with a compromised immune system, vulnerable to any virus or cold germ that may come along. Any of these casual exposures may turn into a severe lung infection and/or pneumonia at the drop of a hat. So we are consistently faced with a reminded of our mortality.' COPD patient, California

for only a few weeks or months, so no long-lasting damage to the reputation of tobacco was sustained. The Popes remained opposed to smoking until the time of Pope Benedict XIII (1649-1730) who, following his adoption of the habit, repealed the relevant papal bulls.

The Greek Orthodox Church, too, banned smoking among the faithful at a time when its flock was resident across most of Eastern Europe. The reason had a biblical slant: the patriarchs claimed that it was tobacco that had intoxicated Noah.

In Berne, Switzerland, the offence of using tobacco was ranked alongside those listed in the ten commandments. It was here that in 1675 the Tobacco Chamber was founded, similar in model to the Papal Inquisition and designed to persecute all users. The Ming emperor in China outlawed its growth and consumption and there were periods of persecution, too, for Japanese smokers.

Fears for the health of smokers quickly spread. Ben Jonson (c1573-1637), in his play *Bartholomew Fair*, wrote, 'The lungs of the tobacconist are rotted, the liver spotted, the brain smoked like the backside of the pig-woman's booth here, and the whole body within black as her pan you saw e'en now without.'

But the fact is that the habit soon caught on, not least because sailors who saw first hand how Indians enjoyed smoking were quick to take it up. During the 16th and 17th centuries seafarers were important figures, admired as heroes and were as much an influence on the young as any of today's soccer stars or baseball players.

Writer Robert Burton (1577-1640) was ambivalent. 'Tobacco, divine, rare, superexcellent tobacco, which goes far beyond all their panaceas, potable gold and philosopher's stones, a sovereign remedy to all diseases'. But on the other hand, 'As it is commonly abused by most men, which take it as tinkers do ale, 'tis a plague, a mischief, a violent purger of goods, lands, health, hellish, devilish and damned tobacco, the ruin and overthrow of body and soul.'

Edmund Spenser (1552-99) also called it 'divine'. In France the comic playwright Molière (1622-73) reflected a growing feeling when he has his hero Don Juan state, 'He who lives without tobacco is not worthy to live.'

The belief that tobacco was a good thing gradually became a commonly held view everywhere. While Peter the Great liberated the smokers of Russia, the Enlightenment obliterated European objections and a general public support for the habit quashed the opposition of Puritans in the colonies, Switzerland and elsewhere.

Given its early ties with the New World and the active patronage of King Philip III, Seville in Spain was destined to become the world's first tobacco town. The production of cigars flourished while the poor used scraps of cigar wrap and a sprinkling of used tobacco to construct the first cigarettes.

Dismayed at seeing the Spanish take a lead, the British were keen to play catch-up and from 1616 tobacco was exported out of the infant American colony. Without it, settlement of the region would have failed, as it had done at Roanoke, Sir Walter Raleigh's failed experiment in the New World.

The story of Virginian tobacco is colourful and intriguing. One settler, John Rolfe (1585–1622), finding the Virginia-grown plant bitter, experimented with seeds and yields. After importing a different variety from the West Indies he helped bring about the mass cultivation of tobacco at an early stage in the history of the colony.

Here was a man working in extreme conditions. Many of the early settlers succumbed to disease and exhaustion. The rest were brow-beaten by the Puritanical regime that had determined that idleness was a crime. It was no picnic in Jamestown, the settlement founded and financed by the newly formed exploitative business, the Virginia Company.

But Rolfe took solace in his scientific experiments and in his marriage to an Indian princess, Pocahontas, the daughter of a chief in charge of a confederation of 30 local tribes. This is, of course, the same Pocahontas who allegedly threw herself across Captain John Smith, the military leader of the newly established Jamestown, to prevent his slaughter by her fellow Indians. She further cemented her relations with settlers by bringing them food when they were starving but the close links were broken after Smith returned to Britain in 1609.

With accord between Europeans and Indians deteriorating, Pocahontas was taken prisoner as whites vainly tried to negotiate a peace settlement.

It was during her spell as captive, when she was converted to Christianity, that she fell in love with Rolfe.

Thanks to the knowledge and skills of his in-laws, Rolfe honed the treatment of tobacco so the end result fitted the tastes of the domestic market in Britain. Such was the demand for tobacco that royal opposition to 'the scurvy weed', manifested in many of the king's officials, didn't stand in its way.

In 1616 the law set down that only one acre could be laid down to tobacco for every two earmarked for corn. The law was disregarded when it became apparent that tobacco yielded six times as much as any other crop for the same amount of labour. Establishment antipathy towards tobacco was also tempered when the Virginian crops began to outweigh those imported from Spain, significant in such a competitive relationship.

Tobacco crops were ferried down the network of Virginian rivers to ocean-going ships. A tremendous trade began across the Atlantic and the prosperity of Jamestown was assured.

With tobacco came the first notions of democracy, tried out with small success in the running of the fledgling Virginia. There wasn't a happy ending for either Pocahontas or Rolfe, however. She fell ill and died during a trip to Britain in 1617 and was buried at St George's Church in Gravesend, Kent. He married again but was killed in an Indian attack on his farm.

Settlers in Maryland also seized upon the virtues of growing tobacco. Living was once again hard for the early colonialists, who faced extremes of weather and the ravages of disease.

> 'The natives wrap the tobacco in a certain leaf, in the manner of a musket formed of paper...and having lighted one end of it, by the other they such, absorb or receive that smoke inside with their breath.'
> Bartholomio de las Casas, Columbus expedition of 1492

Life expectancy was short, with half of all children dying before they reached 20. But the farmers were propped up by tobacco and produced 1,000lb (453kg) per season by the end of the 1630s. One settler, the Reverend Hugh Jones, called it 'our meat, drinke, cloathing and moneys'.

Britain was intent on securing its toehold in America when Spanish and Portuguese rivals had been long established in the New World and it wasn't going to let the small consideration of hostile territory get in the way. People needed, quite literally, to carve out the foundations of settlements from virgin territory.

A labour-intensive business, the British colonialists decided to solve two problems in one by transporting troublesome convicts to America to serve a sentence of labouring on the land. The judiciary was delighted. Until then the options for convicted criminals were limited pretty much to hanging. Taking this route, magistrates appeared stern but not callous and at the same time could rid the mother country of its worst offenders.

Memorable cigarette advertising slogans have included 'Reach for a Lucky instead of a sweet' for Lucky Strike and 'Consulate – gives you a taste of the country'.

Initially, this was not a soft option. When transportation was first introduced in 1597 the trip across the Atlantic was extremely arduous and many perished or were weakened by sickness. However, the science of ship building leapt ahead during the ensuing decades, easing the hardships. Some convicts grew to appreciate the outdoor life overseas, away from the pressures of family, friends and the English class system.

The transport of convicts was erratic during times of war, so plantation owners were sometimes left with inadequate numbers of workers – and not all of those were willing to work. After 1717 it cost the plantation owners £10 ($14.60) for each male and £8 ($11.68) for a female transportee, the money being paid to the transporter. Convicts who had completed their sentence often wanted land of their own as did the indentured servants brought over from Britain to work alongside the prisoners, who would theoretically be freed when their length of service expired.

Plantation owners began to look elsewhere for cheaper, more reliable sources of manpower and encountered the African slave trade. It began in a small way in 1619. John Rolfe recorded in his diary that year, 'There came in a Dutch man-of-warre that sold us 20 negars.' The use of slaves escalated as the century wore on, particularly after slavery was legalized in Virginia in 1661. Between 1690 and 1770 about 100,000 slaves were imported into the region, either from the West Indies or more commonly from Africa. Even prior to 1775 and the War of Independence between America and Britain the transportation of convicts had virtually ceased.

The Chesapeake became the world's main tobacco producer, turning an export of some 65,000lb (30,000kg) to Britain in the 1620s to 38lb million (17.2kg million) by 1700. As America greeted independence it was exporting a massive 220lb million (100kg million) of tobacco. American success consigned the tobacco cultivation carried out by the British in the West Indies to history and left the way clear there for sugar production.

By 1750 about 145,000 slaves – 60 per cent of those in the colony – were at work growing tobacco. However, market dominance in this area was quickly lost to the production of cotton. By the middle of the 19th century cotton was established as America's largest export and was worth more to the economy than all the other exports combined. Now slave ownership was concentrated around cotton production, which was in the American south.

But slaves remained vital on the tobacco plantations. Seeds, which were generally planted a dozen days after Christmas, were transplanted from rich beds into the fields in April by the most skilled slaves. It was their job to assiduously weed the fields, tend the plants and top them to prevent flowering. By September it was time to harvest the leaves which were then left in barns to dry. Planters decided when the leaves were ready for tobacco production, dry but not crumbly. Then the slaves stripped the leaves from the stalk – the most expert could even remove the web of the leaf. It was then stored in containers known as hogsheads to await sale and dispatch. The crop arrived in Europe some 15 months after the seeds first sprouted in the ground. Children as young as nine worked on the plantations and there was no retirement age. Only slaves who were incapacitated by pregnancy or sickness could escape the fields.

Expectation of slave labour was high and was rarely satisfied. The plantation owners largely considered their workforce slack while the slaves tried to snatch a precious few moments of illicit liberty. Punishments for lazy or errant slaves are well documented and generally involved flogging.

Slaves were also subject to sale, a trauma that rent families apart. One Dr Elwood Harvey described a sale of slaves in Virginia in 1846: 'When the horrible truth was revealed to their minds that they were to be sold, and nearest relations and friends parted for ever, the effect was indescribably agonizing. Women snatched up their babes and ran screaming into the huts. Children hid behind the huts and trees and the men stood in mute despair... A few old men were sold at prices from $13 to $25, and it was painful to see old men, bowed with years of toil and suffering, stand up to be the jest of brutal tyrants, and to hear them tell their disease and worthlessness, fearing that they would be bought by traders for the Southern market.

'During the sale, the quarters resounded with cries and lamentations that made my heart ache. A woman was next called by name. She gave her infant one wild embrace before leaving it with an old woman, and hastened mechanically to obey the call; but stopped, threw her arms aloft, screamed, and was unable to move.'

Whether or not the 18th-century dandy in London ever considered the pains and perils associated with the tobacco in his pouch or snuff box no one knows.

However, tobacco was key to the success of America both as a colony and as a country in its own right. It was tobacco that helped finance the War of Independence against Britain that began in 1775. The Americans secured loans from the French, using tobacco as collateral.

When the 13 American states were free of British rule tobacco cultivation spread to Kentucky, Tennessee, North Carolina, Ohio, and Missouri. Tobacco leaves were now cured over a wood fire, which better preserved them for export. The taste of tobacco was further enhanced when wood fires were replaced by charcoal.

As quickly as 1794 the infant American government hit upon the idea of raising revenue via tobacco and it was duly taxed by Congress. Further charges were levied in 1862 to help pay for the costly Civil War.

Back in England smoking remained a feature of everyday existence. A gentleman on the Canterbury coach enlightened Charles Dickens's *David Copperfield*, ' 'Orses and dogs is some men's fancy. They're whittles and drink to me – lodging, wife and children – reading, writing and 'rithmetic – snuff, tobacker, and sleep.'

A widespread tolerance of smoking still prevailed. Its reputation was largely unassailable. According to novelist Edward Bulwer-Lytton (1803-73), 'The man who smokes thinks like a sage and acts like a Samaritan'.

The nuts and bolts of smoking were to become much easier. The first specialist tobacco shop was opened in England in 1847 by Philip Morris. Within two years the door had opened on a similar establishment in St Louis, in the US. Three years after that came the invention of matches, which meant the process of lighting up was infinitely easier.

The demand for cigarettes above cigars and snuff first revealed itself after the Crimean War (1853-56), when droves of British soldiers learned from their Turkish allies the joyful convenience of a cigarette. Indeed, it was Scottish veteran Robert Peacock Gloag who opened the first cigarette factory in England in 1856. In the same year a debate about the health implications of tobacco usage began in *The Lancet*, the journal of Britain's medical establishment.

In 1864 the first American cigarette factory had opened its doors, signalling the age of mass-production techniques on both sides of the Atlantic. Later, the Bonsack automatic rolling machine, patented in 1881, did the work of 40 people and enabled tobacco companies to exploit it to their advantage.

In Britain, tobacco was lumped in the 'evils' category by temperance movements, which strove mainly to stop alcohol and alcoholics. There was, however, little evidence that people would reel about or become incapable on tobacco, as Norman Kerr, President of the Society for the Study of Inebriety, conceded in 1888: 'Though no defender of tobacco, which it cannot be denied is a mere luxury, injurious to the health of many even when used in moderation, I am driven to the conclusion that in the philosophical and practical meaning of the term there is no true tobacco inebreity or mania.' In that same year in Britain, five 'Wild Woodbine' cost a penny while a loaf of best bread was selling for sixpence.

> 'How marriage ruins a man! It is as demoralizing as cigarettes and far more expensive.' Oscar Wilde

The age of cigarettes was not uniformly welcomed in America, either. One New York school commissioner of the 1890s described his misgivings like this: 'Many a bright lad has had his will power weakened, his moral principle sapped, his nervous system wrecked, and his whole life spoiled before he is 17 years old by the detested cigarette.

'The cigarette fiend in time becomes a liar and a thief. He will commit petty thefts to get money to feed his insatiable appetite for nicotine. He lies to his parents, his teachers and his best friends. He neglects his studies and, narcotized by nicotine, sits at his desk half stupefied, his desire for work, his ambition, dulled if not dead.'

In 1882, in his book *The Use Of Tobacco*, John Hinds wrote, 'No man who smokes daily can be said to be at any time in perfect health.'

During that decade there were a variety of state laws introduced to restrict the sale and consumption of cigarettes.

As the 19th-century gave way to the 20th, however, the smoking habit among Australians had reached phenomenal proportions. They consumed about 3lb (1.36kg) of tobacco per year per head, more than double the figure of those in the United Kingdom where people smoked some 1.41lb (0.64kg) each. Most Antipodean smokers still preferred a pipe.

Australian cartoonist Norman Lindsay explained, 'Tobacco in those days was a cult and the pipe its holy symbol. Religious frenzy was exploded over the virtues of briars, clays, meerschaums, cherry-wood, corn cobs or even German porcelain bowls with a yard of cherry-wood stem. Friendships barely survived conflict of opinion of whether dry or damp tobacco smokes best, and brands of tobacco were discussed as gourmets acclaim rare vintages.

In 1908 a Sydney department store offered its most exotic pipe for 13s3 while the cheapest cherry-woods were running out between 3d and 8d each. This was considerably cheaper than pipe tobacco at the time, which cost about 6s 3d per pound. For the Australian market pipe stems were strengthened with silver so they were more durable in the bush.

In Japan, where tobacco products fell under state control in 1898, there was a growing concern about the effects of smoking on the young. In 1900 a law was introduced banning anyone under the age of 20 from smoking.

In 1907 the British Medical Association heard from GP Dr Herbert Tidswell about the poisonous habit of smoking. He suggested that every

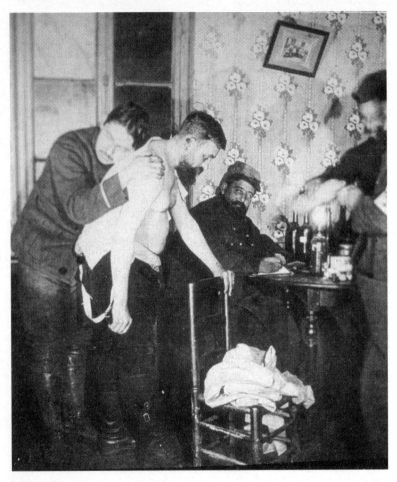

Early medical examination: a doctor listening for lung disease by placing his ear on a man's back.

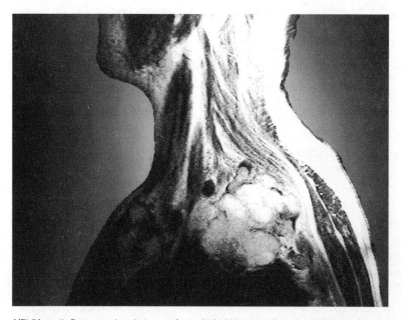

MRI (Magnetic Resonance Imaging) scan of a sagittal (side) section through a patient's neck and chest, showing a malignant tumour in the right lung apex. Cancer cells divide rapidly and chaotically, often clumping together to form tumours (as seen here), which invade and destroy surrounding tissues. Lung cancer causes a cough, chest pain, shortness of breath, and weight loss. If the cancer has not spread (metastasized) to other tissues, the tumour may be removed surgically. Other treatments include chemotherapy and radiotherapy.

girl and boy in Britain should be encouraged to sign a pledge preventing them from taking up the habit. And he highlighted the risks of cancer of the tongue and lip. Tidswell was echoed by Dr I Adler in 1912 who believed smoking was linked to lung cancer. However, both were opposed by other doctors who argued that no clear case had been presented against moderate use of tobacco.

Mixed messages were the order of the day. In 1923 scientists in Paris claimed that smoking was beneficial because nicotine formed chemicals that would fight bacterial infections while in Germany doctors were concerned about the effects of nicotine.

Claims by an eminent British surgeon in 1926 that tobacco caused cancer of the tongue were countered by an International Tobacco Exhibition held in London the following year at which a different doctor insisted there was 'no risk of cancer from tobacco'.

In 1932 London doctors once again publicly criticized the young for slimming, smoking, and drinking too much. This may have been as much a knee-jerk response of Britain's strong puritan vein as genuine fears for young people's health.

There's evidence that if the prohibition of alcohol had succeeded in America after 1919, smokers would have been next on the agenda. Evangelist Billy Sunday (1862–1935), who spoke out against the evils of liquor, was quoted as saying, somewhat prematurely, 'Prohibition is won, now for tobacco.'

Of course, Prohibition failed because of the public desire to sidestep the law. Undoubtedly the same outcome would have occurred if tobacco had been the target of the legislature.

The tobacco industry was in turn robust in defence of its products. In 1933 an advertisement for Chesterfields began, 'Just as pure as the water you drink...and practically untouched by human hands.' Only history would prove those naïve claims to be misguided.

Following the claim by German doctors that smokers who inhaled absorbed eight times more nicotine than those who did not, doctors in Nazi Germany were among the first to research the link between lung cancer and cigarettes. The result was a report in 1939 by Franz Hermann Muller from the University of Cologne, entitled *Tobacco Misuse And Lung Carcinoma*. Adolf Hitler (1889–1945) was famously finnicky about living a healthy lifestyle, although he kept his dependence on prescribed drugs very much under wraps. No one was permitted to smoke in his presence and he even invested a considerable sum of his own money into an 'Institute for the Struggle against Tobacco'.

Hitler launched the first anti-smoking campaign in the world and magazines and newspapers were loud with warnings of the dangers of cigarettes. One magazine asked, 'Brother national socialist, do you know that our Fuhrer is against smoking and thinks that every German is responsible to the whole people for all his deeds and emissions and does not have the right to damage his body with drugs?'

Lucky Strike went white in 1942 when the war effort demanded the titanium in its familiar green ink. The wartime packet's sole concession to colour was a red bull's eye. Sales of the patriotic cigarette rose by 38 per cent.

Women were forbidden to buy cigarettes in cafés and smoking was banned in many public places. Students – and their teachers – were forbidden to smoke. Pregnant women and the men of the Luftwaffe were also prohibited from indulging. There was even an attempt to limit smoking among soldiers. Tobacco advertising was restricted, too, and non-smokers were seen as ideal Aryans, clean-living members of the master race. These efforts were supervised by Heinrich Himmler (1900–45), Hitler's unattractive henchman, once described as a 'sadistic authoritarian who developed a passion for unlimited control over others'.

However, Himmler's ardent two-pronged attack on smokers, through legislation and propaganda, was a dismal failure. The number of smokers in fascist Germany rose in the same way as it did in other European countries, proof, if any were needed, that even a forcefully delivered, uniform 'smoking kills' message is not effective.

More than that, his anti-smoking stance has permitted pro-smoking groups to label any measures to curb the habit as 'health fascism'. Even the most ardent anti-smokers are not keen to be bracketed in their outlook alongside Hitler.

The role of tobacco in society was dramatically altered by the two World Wars that scarred the 20th century. Tobacco in general and cigarettes in particular carved for themselves a niche in the psyche of soldiers. As one Second World War veteran remembered, 'Lots of people who went into the army as non-smokers were smoking by the time they had finished their training. Often you heard the call "fall out for a smoke". Everybody sat around the barrack square and brought out a cigarette. There was nothing else to do.'

Recollections of incidents in the Wars are often recited in the context of cigarettes, the smoking of them or the lack of them.

In September 1914 Captain JC Dunn recorded how British soldiers kept in good spirits, despite the privations of the front line in France.

'By far their chief grouse was the lack of cigarettes, of which they ran out early; the few packets of 'Caporal' I had been able to get for my own people were not an efficient substitute for "Woodbines" – "fags". We had not been seriously engaged, for all that we had been in the thick of all that had taken place. Such things as hot food, rest and the minor stimulant of tobacco had been unobtainable and no one could have removed his boots for more than a few minutes at a time. When these facts are considered, the morale of the men was really extraordinary.'

In the same month Brigadier-General EL Spears witnessed the execution of a French soldier guilty of deserting his post. The officer in charge of the stressful incident was General de Maud'huy.

'The sound of a volley in the distance announced that all was over. General de Maud'huy wiped the beads of perspiration from his brow, and for the first time perhaps his hand trembled as he lit his pipe.'

Edwin Campion Vaughan, of the Warwickshire Regiment, served at the Battle of Langemarck in August 1917. An officer was stretchered into the pillbox he was defending.

' "Where are you hit?" I asked.

' "In the back near the spine. Could you shift my gas helmet from under me?"

'I cut away the satchel and dragged it out; then he asked for a cigarette. Dunham produced one and he put it between his lips; I struck a match and held it across, but the cigarette had fallen on his chest and he was dead.'

Moments later Vaughan produced a box of 100 Abdulla Egyptian cigarettes which he had been conserving in his rucksack. Like other British officers, he sought to raise the spirits of his men by supplying extra smokes paid for out of his own pocket. 'I had just opened the box when there was a rattle of rifles outside and a voice yelled. "Germans coming over, sir!" Cigarettes went flying into the water (on the ground) as I hurled myself through the doorway and ran forward into the darkness where my men were firing.'

Cigarettes formed part of the soldiers' rations but the amount of tobacco was never sufficient and could be supplemented when possible at outlets like the Expeditionary Force Canteen. Loved ones sent cigarettes from home and newspapers launched tobacco funds to extend supply even further. A reluctance to smoke cigarettes, detectable before the war, was obliterated. Its ability to suppress the appetite as well as its calming effect was all to the good when men were faced with appalling privation and ceaseless shelling.

As General John Pershing (1860–1948), commander of the American Expeditionary Force in France after the US involvement in 1917, observed, 'You ask me what we need to win this war, I answer tobacco, as much as bullets. Tobacco is as indispensable as the daily ration. We must have thousands of tons of it without delay.'

It was during the hellish years of trench warfare that one of the most enduring superstitions about cigarettes sprang up and even today people will refuse the third light from a match. The theory was that enemy snipers saw the first light, took aim on the second light and fired on the third. Soldiers began to smoke with their fingers around the filter end and the butt facing into the palm so that enemy soldiers in trenches close by would not be able to identify targets.

After the war the love affair with nicotine continued. Japan celebrated the end of First World War hostilities with the creation of 'Peace' cigarettes. By 1928 the United States was producing 100 billion cigarettes each year to satisfy demand. In 1931 came the introduction of cellophane on cigarette packets to help keep them fresh. Nothing, it seemed, would stop the success story that was tobacco. As one observer noted, non-smokers at the time were 'a feeble and ever-dwindling minority'. 'The hopeless nature of their struggle becomes plain when we remember that all countries, whatever their form of government, now encourage and facilitate the passion for smoking in every conceivable way, merely for the sake of the revenue which it produces... If we consider how in the past the efforts of the most absolute despots the world has ever seen were powerless to stop the spread of smoking we may rest assured that any such attempts today, when the habit has grown to such gigantic dimensions, can result only in a miserable fiasco.'

> In 1860 workers at Lorillard put $100 bills randomly into packets of Century cigarettes to celebrate the company's centenary.

Nicotine became more significant than ever following the start of the Second World War. Few servicemen escaped the lure of the cigarette, which became central to their existence.

For many their recollections of the war revolved around cigarettes and smoking, a time when the popular brands included Woodbines, Camel, Lucky Strike, and Pall Mall.

Arthur Stephenson, of the Royal Artillery, has one painful memento from his service in North Africa. 'I've got a lighter at home with a Canadian badge on it. In the desert I was trying to light my pipe. This Canadian came up and went to light it for me. He was there one minute and gone the next. A shell-burst killed him outright. All that was left was his lighter. He was only three yards away from me and I was completely unscathed.'

The German pilot of a Messerschmitt, shot down into a Tunisian wheat field and taken prisoner by the British soldiers he had been shooting at, sought solace in a smoke. Serviceman Alan Moorehead witnessed the scene: 'As they searched the German, he fumbled for a cigarette and made motions for someone to light it for him. He did this mechanically and without attempting to speak, and the hand which held the cigarette was shaking badly.

'Someone lit the cigarette and for some reason I could not understand the man with the pistol motioned the pilot to a place in the wheat about 20 yards from the fallen plane. Then, quite accidentally, everyone stepped back from the pilot at the same time and he was left along standing in the wild flowers.

'You could see very clearly what he was thinking. He was thinking, "They are going to shoot me now. This is the end. The one with the pistol will fire at my body." He stiffened and the hand holding the cigarette was tensed and shivering. Little beades of sweat came out in a line on his forehead and he looked straight ahead.

'All this took only a moment and then, in the same involuntary way, the British troops moved toward him again and motioned him to march with them back toward the road.

'The pilot did not comprehend for a moment. Then he relaxed and drew deeply on his cigarette and it was again quite clear that he was saying to himself in a spasm of half-understood relief, "It's all right. They are not going to shoot me..." This actual physical contact with the pilot, his shock and his fear, suddenly made one conscious that we were fighting human beings and not just machines and hilltops and guns.'

Actor Anthony Quayle was with General Sir Noel Mason-MacFarlane on Gibraltar when French bombers attacked in reprisal for the sinking of the French fleet at Toulon on 3 July 1940.

'I remember the attack because I was having lunch with Mason-Mac in his house when the planes came. We quickly dived into a cupboard under the stairs as bombs fell all round the house. Mason-Mac took a cigarette from his case just as a bomb landed so close to the house that the whole building shook. It made him jump and he dropped the case and all the cigarettes spilled all over the floor. Those are the funny things you remember about the war.'

Even amid the horror of the Nazi concentration camp at Auschwitz where hundreds of thousands of Jews were killed in gas chambers, cigarettes gave a spark of hope. British-born Leon Greenman was deported from Holland to the camp in Poland where his wife and baby son perished. But he remembered, 'In Auschwitz, I was the only Englishman and often tried to seek the company of the British prisoners of war held nearby. Some gave me cigarettes that I could trade for an extra bowl of watery camp soup.'

When actress Marlene Dietrich paraded through Rome in a jeep shortly after the city fell to the Allies she was given an uproarious reception. 'It was like an Easter Parade. The boys threw cigarettes and chocolate,' she recalled later.

In India British serviceman Fred Leonard remembers the rousingly named Victory V cigarettes: 'They were horrible things. I was practically a non-smoker when I went into the army. As teenagers we would buy five cigarettes out of a machine for two pennies and hand them around but smoking was very much weekends only for me. But by the time I left the army I was hooked, and remained so for years afterwards.'

Margaret Freyer was a survivor of the bombing of Dresden, which was completely destroyed by a fire storm on St Valentine's Day 1945. During the conflagration she encountered a soldier. 'Then he started to weep. He continued to stroke my back, mumbling words about bravery, Russian campaign...but this here, this is hell. I don't grasp his meaning and offer him a cigarette.'

A British prisoner of war was taken to a Red Cross representative holed up in a German Baroness's mansion in the last weeks of the Second World War. 'He was a Swiss national and seemed a furtive type. We eyed him with suspicion, he seemed much too concerned with the Baroness. However, he did issue us with some Red Cross food and cigarettes, which helped save the situation, though we noted that the Baroness was also smoking fairly heavily.

After the mansion was taken over by Russian troops, the liberated prisoners discovered a locked cabinet. 'Inside the sideboard we found a huge stock of cigarettes, cigars and pipe tobacco. He [the overseer] must have been a good Nazi, considering how scarce these commodities were in Germany.'

As Berlin fell resident Claus Fuhrmann recalled the desperation of the citizens. 'While bullets were whistling through the air they scrambled for a tin of fish or a pouch of tobacco.' Cigarettes even became currency in the chaos of post-war Germany.

During the execution of Nazi war criminals at Nuremburg in 1946, two men were hanged and eight were awaiting their fate when there came a special request. 'The American colonel directing the executions asked the American general representing the United States on the Allied Control Commission if those present could smoke. An affirmative answer brought cigarettes into the hands of almost every one of the 30-odd persons present.' They smoked as two bodies dangled on ropes below the floor of the scaffolding.

After the Second World War cigarettes still remained an important feature of forces life, particularly among conscripts. Gerry Dance joined the Royal Air Force in 1950 for national service and remembered the period fondly. 'We developed great friendships and camaraderie, like sharing a pack of Woodbines during breaks in drill, even cutting them in half. On four shillings [20p/22¢] a day we could not afford to each buy a pack.'

Meanwhile, Hollywood was finding a further use for cigarettes in the motion pictures of the '30s, '40s, '50s, and '60s. Stars quite literally smouldered as they contemplated relations with an amour and the cigarette became a ready metaphor for sex.

Film makers were wrestling with the proprieties of the Hays Code, formally introduced in 1930 to control the content of films. There was to be no nudity, ridicule of the clergy, inference of sexual perversion or the sale of women's virtues. But while these, and the illegal trafficking of drugs, could not be portrayed in films smoking could.

One of the finest examples of a cigarette meaning much more than just a smoke comes in the 1942 film *Now, Voyager* starring Bette Davis (1908–99) as a frustrated spinster saved from nervous collapse by a kindly psychiatrist. She emerges as a butterfly from her caterpillar existence, only to embark on a doomed love affair with a married man, played by Paul Henreid.

The first glimpse of the dowdy Davis shows her as a secret smoker (to rebel against her domineering mother and as a kind of sex-replacement therapy). She is largely a prisoner in her bedroom where she nervously carves intricate patterns on cigarette boxes made from ivory.

Later, the married man she falls for acquires the fond habit of lighting two cigarettes at a time, one for himself and one for Davis. Inevitably, she draws on the cigarette with heavy lidded eyes, wearing a look of naked

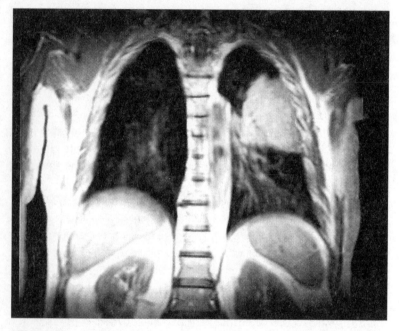

MRI scan of a coronal (frontal) section through a patient's chest, showing a malignant tumour in the left lung.

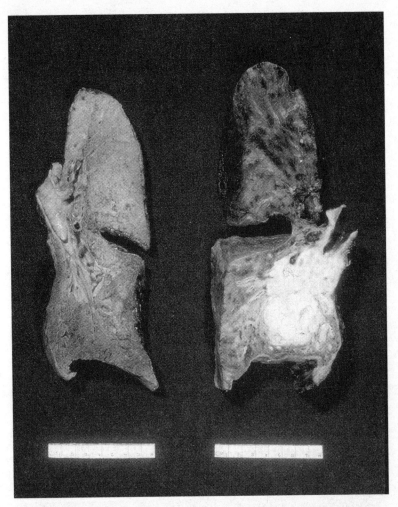

Post-mortem specimens of a sectioned normal lung (LEFT) and a lung destroyed by bronchial cancer (RIGHT). The tumour appears as a white mass in the lower lobe, while tissue in the upper lobe is blackened by tar deposits from the cigarette smoking. The lung at the left shows some blackening, possibly from environmental soot or more moderate smoking. Cancer of the bronchus often arises from smoking, especially cigarettes, and there is a marked association between dose (number of cigarettes smoked) and risk of developing the disease. Mortality in lung cancer is high, as the disease has often metastasized (spread) before it is detected.

desire. The film communicates precisely the nature of their relationship without so much as a glimpse of pale flesh.

Like other actresses of her generation, Davis also employed the gravel voice that often signifies a smoker with great effect.

In the same year *Casablanca* was made, a movie described as 'cinema par excellence' by film critic Leslie Halliwell and one of the most frequently repeated films on TV. The film is set in the Moroccan city of the title where hundreds of refugees from the Second World War tried to purloin papers in order to travel to the US. Inspired by an unproduced play written by a man who had witnessed the refugee crisis unfolding in Europe at the beginning of the war, the action takes place primarily in Rick's Café Americain.

Rick, of course, is played by Humphrey Bogart, canny, cruel and trembling with repressed emotion. The audience first sees him hunched over a chess board, smoking a cigarette, cool and clever. His dapper image is confirmed by the appearance early on of a sleek, silvery cigarette case. Afterwards he is almost always pictured with cigarette in hand, indeed, he delivers some of his most ascerbic lines with a tube of tobacco dangling from his lips. Somewhat bizarrely, the white tuxedo that he wears throughout never seems yellowed by cigarette smoke nor is it peppered with burn marks from flying ash. Ah well.

It's not just him, though. Piano player Sam, played by Dooley Wilson, inevitably has a cigarette burning above the keyboard. Peter Lorre, playing the ill-fated Ugarte, Claude Rains, as Captain Louis Renault and Paul Henreid, as the heroic Victor Laszlo, are all pictured smoking copiously. The air in Rick's café is consequently heavy with smoke from cigarettes and hookahs.

The only apparent non-smoker is Ilse Lund, played by the translucent beauty Ingrid Bergman. Married to Laszlo and in love with Rick, she finds herself in clinches with both and is clearly never put off by what must have been an overwhelming stench of tobacco.

Made a decade before real alarm about the effects of smoking began to spread, *Casablanca*, a film that imprinted itself on the psyche of the Western world for generations, was literally played out in a smoke haze. If only there was 'smellavision', the favourable public response to the masterpiece might have been tempered.

By the first half of the 20th century cigarette smoking – and thus smoke inhalation – had become widespread. But just as smoking was on the rise so were the instances of lung cancer. Britain was bowing under one of the highest rates in the world. In 1940 the death rate in America from lung cancer was more than treble that of 1933. Epidemiology, the study of the distribution and causes of disease, had until then been largely confined to infectious afflictions. Lung cancer and heart disease were virgin territory as far as this kind of science was concerned. But, as the whispers of anxiety about the effects of smoking began to grow ever louder, epidemiologists were irresistibly drawn into the arena.

At the end of the Second World War a medical symposium at the University of Buffalo in the US was pondering the possible link of tobacco to lung cancer. The primary indication was that lung cancer incidence in men was six times that of women. However, it seemed that a post-war increase in the number of smokers had swung the balance towards women, proving that smoking was connected to lung cancer. Doctors remained cautious, however, for fear of causing unnecessary alarm.

The post-war cigarette industry remained buoyant. One of the first popular television programmes in America, 'Your Hit Parade', was sponsored by 'Lucky Strike'. Other popular brands were Kent, Winston, and Salem, the first filter-tipped menthol cigarette. A majority of people smoked and more women were smoking than ever before.

Disquiet about the effects of cigarettes on the body rumbled on like distant thunder. Although smoking had always evoked strong feelings those against it worked mainly on instinct. It was time for modern science to be brought into play to put smoking in its box, once and for all.

But when it came, the revelation about lung cancer and its link to cigarettes was far from an overnight sensation. It took a two-pronged offensive – out of Britain and America – over a decade to establish as fact the hazards of smoking. The main players in the scientific world in Britain were Sir Richard Doll and Sir Austin Bradford Hill. In America German-born Ernst Wynder (1922–99), who fled to the US with his family to escape Nazi persecution, is credited with pioneering work that established a connection.

Post-war Britain was suffering calamitous levels of lung cancer – about 80 per cent of men smoked – but no one was entirely sure why the disease prevailed. In 1949 Sir Richard Doll and Sir Austin Bradford Hill produced findings that appeared to prove smoking was linked to lung cancer. 'The secretary at the Medical Research Council was quite convinced of our conclusion, that smoking was the principal cause of lung cancer. He told us that this would have a big public response,' recalled Doll. But their data related only to the London area. They were asked to spread the net to see if the same results could be culled from elsewhere.

By 1951 the results were mirrored in five cities nationwide and Doll's ground-breaking work appeared to be underpinned. 'Contrary to expect-

'Within countries such as the UK and the US, tobacco use is much more prevalent amongst people with serious mental disorders such as schizophrenia or among those incarcerated in prisons. This in itself should not be interpreted as strong evidence that smoking causes stress or poor mental health, since it is possible that these individuals use tobacco primarily in an attempt to reduce their stress. However, other evidence is consistent with the idea that being a smoker may increase stress and that, in the longer term, quitting actually decreases stress.' Royal College of Physicians

ations, it made no impact. It was reported always with qualification. Somebody was put up by the tobacco industry to say it wasn't proved, it was just statistics,' said Doll.

Even fellow cancer researchers were reluctant to accept Doll's findings because they were not accustomed to using epidemiological studies to find out the cause of non-infectious diseases. In 1954 Health Minister Iain Macleod met the press to issue a watered-down warning about smoking and its attendant dangers. Chain-smoking throughout, Macleod thanked Doll and Hill for 'what little information we have' and went on to announce a headline-grabbing donation by the tobacco industry to the Medical Research Council. There seemed little prospect at this stage of official measures to restrict the activities of the tobacco industry.

But, seeing the lie of the land, tobacco companies introduced filter tips in the 1950s to reassure smokers they were being protected from the harmful elements of cigarettes. The industry tried to go further, introducing synthetic tobacco substitutes into cigarettes in order to reduce toxicity. However, the new products bombed and were withdrawn.

Realizing he had to convince scientists before gaining the confidence of the public, Doll undertook another more major task, studying the smoking habits of some 40,000 British doctors, this time working with Sir Richard Peto. They had to play a waiting game. The aim was to see who developed lung cancer out of this massive cohort and whether or not they were smokers. Even initial findings appeared to illustrate a link between smoking and incidences of lung cancer.

By 1956 the percentage of smoking doctors suffering from lung cancer seemed substantial enough to justify faith in the premise. Yet still there were lingering doubts. Two statisticians, one British and one American, maintained that the figures did not imply smoking caused lung cancer. One believed that there was a genetic reason behind people choosing to smoke and that a similar genetic flaw was responsible for lung cancer. This was later proved to be false.

Only in 1957 did the government ask the Medical Research Council for advice on the findings. Briefed on Doll and Peto's findings and on studies emerging from America the Council was at last prepared to endorse the 'smoking causes lung cancer' message. The scientific issue was at last settled.

Yet even then there was a reluctance to accept the findings. There still remained a battle for the hearts and minds of the public. It wasn't until the Royal College of Physicians published a report called *Smoking And Health* in 1962 that a furore over smoking finally broke out.

'It wasn't until the media themselves changed their minds – journalists and TV presenters were often smokers – that the public began to be convinced. By this time doctors had nearly all given up. Media coverage about the doubts continued until the early 1970s with the media giving disproportionate weight to the tobacco industry side,' remembered Doll who himself quit smoking after writing his very first report in 1949. (He says, 'I didn't find it hard to give up. It just seemed silly. I was convinced it caused nasty diseases so I just stopped doing it. I was not addicted, smoking for me was just a habit. However, my wife found it exceptionally difficult to give up.')

Doll's findings had been echoed constantly by Wynder in America. Even before winning his medical degree, Wynder had been captivated by the subject of lung cancer. He was present at an autopsy as part of his studies and was intrigued to see that the lungs of the dead man under the knife were blackened. Only later when he spoke to the widow did he realize that the man smoked two packets of cigarettes a day. He was determined to discover more and persuaded thoracic surgeon Evarts Graham to give him access to numerous records. Graham, a heavy smoker, reluctantly agreed. Wynder compared some 649 lung cancer patients with 600 controls and decided that the incidence of lung cancer was 40 times higher in smokers. In 1950 his work was published in the *Journal Of The American Medical Association*. Public awareness was dramatically raised when a feature called 'Cancer By The Carton' was published in *Reader's Digest* in 1952.

All the while Wynder continued his research. In 1953 he produced a landmark report showing that mice that had had their backs painted with cigarette tar developed tumours. It was the first biological link that connected smoking and cancer although the experiments were dogged with criticism from those who remained sceptical. A year later, another *Reader's Digest* article, 'The Cigarette Controversy', brought discussion into the public domain.

In 1957 Surgeon General Leroy Edgar Burney (1906–98) became the first federal official to name smoking as a cause of lung cancer. In the same year Evarts Graham, the unlikely champion of the anti-smoking lobby, died of lung cancer. Convinced by Wynder's work, he quit the habit five years earlier, but it was not, as he noted in a letter to Wynder, early enough.

Doll published his survey on doctors' smoking in 1964, the same year that the US Surgeon General produced his first report *Smoking And Health*. It was a united front that could no longer be ignored. Tobacco companies mobilized, continually sowing seeds of doubt about the effect of cigarette smoking and clinging to the fact that a minority of scientists still believed 'tobacco is innocent'.

Oscar Auerbach conducted his controversial 'smoking beagles' laboratory experiment in 1967, in which about 90 dogs had holes cut in their throats so they could wear special smoking collars. Some smoked filter tipped, some smoked untipped, while a control group smoked nothing at all. After 875 days, the surviving dogs were killed and opened up to search for evidence of lung cancer. Auerbach had already carried out analysis of cells from the bronchial tubes of cadavers, which indicated that smoking caused lung cancer. As expected, smoking dogs did show signs of lung cancer, but the results were not conclusive.

Nevertheless, a 1970 internal memorandum at the tobacco company Gallaher – made public by the American policy of document disclosure – proved the results were telling.

'One of the striking features of the Auerbach experiment was that practically every dog which smoked suffered significantly from the effects of smoke either in terms of severe irritation and bronchitis, pre-cancerous changes or cancer.'

The beagles were subjected to excessive doses of smoke but nevertheless the memo concluded, 'We believe that the Auerbach work proves beyond reasonable doubt that fresh whole smoke is carcinogenic to dog lungs and therefore it is highly likely that it is carcinogenic to human lungs.' The admission was, of course, privately made and not publicly broadcast.

Graphic designer Bruce Aiken recalls a smoking career that was born, survived and died during this historic time for the tobacco industry: 'I started smoking when I was about nine years old, with a friend. We were too young to buy cigarettes so we went around to his parents' house and sorted through lots of dog ends that they had left in the ashtray. We would take them apart and use the contents inside a cigarette paper to make our own cigarettes. There wasn't much nicotine or tar in them.

'When I was aged 13 local shop keepers would break a packet of cigarettes up. They would sell them in paper bags in ones, twos or threes. You could buy them with your pocket money although it was against the law. I progressed from buying loose cigarettes to a packet of Dominoes that contained three cigarettes, which were longer and fatter than Woodbines. These were obviously aimed at people who had little money.

'The other option was rolling your own after buying half an ounce of Golden Virginia or Old Holborn. We used to split a cigarette paper lengthways so that there wasn't so much paper and it could be smoked in one breath.

'When I was a teenager there was a party at my house when my parents were on holiday. During the party I found a cigarette that had drink spilled on it. Knowing there would be no cigarettes left in the morning – there never were when you were a teenager – I carefully put it on a radiator to dry. The next morning the outside paper looked wrinkly but felt dry so I held a match to it and sucked. The middle of it was still wet and a mixture of nicotine, tar, and stale drink filled my mouth. It was revolting.'

A row about sponsorship erupted in Britain after tennis player Martina Navratilova was seen wearing a tennis kit bearing a 'Kim' logo. The effectiveness of voluntary agreements controlling tobacco advertising was called into question.

In the '50s Aiken would visit holiday camps with his family. 'There was only one serving of breakfast and we were all woken up at the same time by messages booming over the tannoy. I can clearly remember starting the day with this song ringing in my ears: "Today's cigarette is a Capstan. The great cigarette is a Capstan. A real cool flavour that you'll never forget, Capstan - it's today's cigarette." '

In the '60s there were more brands available than ever before. 'The stronger the cigarette that you smoked, the more of a man you were. There was Gold Flake in an almost orange packet, which was lethally strong. To be cool you would smoke Disc Bleu. If you were super cool you would smoke Gitanes. The ultra cool among us smoked Gitanes Menthe.' With a professional interest in the advertising industry Aiken remembers the first professionally redesigned cigarette packet, Guards. However, during the hippy era young people refused to smoke a brand that was associated with the army so the redesign had little impact.

'It was in the '60s that I switched to tipped cigarettes. That is when we first started thinking about the dangers of smoking. Apart from tipped cigarettes we smoked Galoises because they were made from air-dried tobacco and there was allegedly less tar in them even though they were incredibly strong. And we smoked roll-ups. The advantage was that there was no saltpetre in the paper which is why a roll-up would go out. It burnt at a lower degree and so reduced the intake of tar and nicotine. That's what we believed, anyway.

'Later in the same decade we started going on package holidays. Suddenly we found unbelievably cheap cigarettes abroad. In Spain there were very badly made cigarettes called Celtas. They cost a tiny amount but they were so poorly produced that you had to keep your cigarette horizontal while you were lighting it or the tobacco would fall out.

'It was a commonly held belief that when you brought cigarettes back into the country the restrictions applied only to unopened packets. Consequently I used to return from holiday with a suitcase full of cigarette packets, all open and missing two.'

By the 1970s some companies were taking a stance on the smoking issue. Airlines including Finnair and BOAC (which became British Airways) provided non-smoking areas on flights. Rank Leisure ensured that a section of seats in its British cinemas were the preserve of those who chose not to smoke. But it was a long while before these were smoke-less zones. Non-smokers watched helplessly as clouds drifted towards them, sent up by the smokers on the other side of the room or cabin.

The first tar and nicotine tables were published in April 1973. The average tar yield of cigarettes then on sale was 20.6mg. Within a year the tar tables classified brands into high, middle-to-high, middle, low-to-middle and low categories.

Aiken smoked throughout the '80s. 'It was wonderful to have something to do with your hands while you were talking to people. I have never found a substitute.'

He decided to give up when he realized smoking was affecting his health. 'I ran swiftly up the stairs to read my kids a story – and did not have the breath to start the book for two or three minutes. Probably for the first time, I realized smoking was seriously hindering my lung power.' Until that point, the volume of anti-smoking sentiments, growing ever louder, had had no effect.

'I remember a doctor friend of ours who said, "By the time I get cancer they will have found a cure." The long-term health consequences of smoking were not really a consideration.

'Every time I gave up smoking previously I ended up allowing myself just one after dinner. Within days I was back to 20 a day. Now I approach it as an alcoholic would a drink. I gave up smoking but I am still a smoker. I tell myself I can have a cigarette any time I want one as long as I know that I cannot just have one.'

04 HEALTH

What do Walt Disney, baseball star Babe Ruth, Britain's King George VI and Beach Boy Carl Wilson all have in common? They died from lung cancer probably induced by smoking. In turn, they are linked to literally millions of others, famous, unremarkable, rich, poor, loved, and lonely who have surrendered their health to nicotine addiction. To the frustration of the anti-smoking lobby and the friends and family left behind, their deaths – along with other smoking-related problems – are largely avoidable. That's why tobacco use has been branded a 'man-made plague'.

There are some people who insist that smoking does not cause lung cancer. These are presumably the same conspiracy theorists who claim that man never landed on the moon (it was all staged in the film studios), that Kennedy is not dead (he is living in a vegetable-like state on a Greek island), and that Elvis is alive and well and peers out of windows at visitors to his Graceland home in Memphis.

According to the Australian Council on Smoking and Health there have been 57,000 studies that have stated 'smoking is bad for you' – and this is probably a conservative estimate. Can they all be wrong?

But that minority of folk who feel that smoking is only a shade more hazardous that eating fruit gums have a point. The 'smoking kills' scenario is not as straightforward as it seems.

Few of us have the know-how to distinguish a sound and well-observed scientific study from a shoddy one. There's plenty at issue as one study deconstructs the next, one uses this set of figures while another uses that one. Some are drawn up after scrutiny of fat bundles of data, others use a quota that is decidedly slim. A number of studies have been made on humans, many on animals. Some statistics are produced by men in white coats whose wages are paid by the tobacco companies. Still more are financed by the anti-smoking lobby. Reports can be biased, imprecise, and emotive, and some pose more questions than they answer. Sometimes science can be misused and abused. In short, some headline figures are more credible than others – but the staunch-and-steadfast type are difficult to tell apart from the ropey, don't-waste-your-time-and-emotions sort. It's tricky to gauge a reasonable response to newspaper stories that seize on sensational scientific sound-bites.

So you read some features on the dangers of smoking and with one puff you can virtually feel them tying the tag to your big toe and wheeling you off to the big freeze in the morgue. In response, there is literature which implies the risks are minimal, that smoking is shouldering the statistical burden for conditions like obesity, diabetes, and so forth and that, anyway, you have a right to live life as you please. An article published in 1998 accused the US government of grossly inflating the number of smoking casualties. Called 'Lies, Damned Lies, And 400,000 Smoking-Related Deaths', the authors decided that 'the war on smoking...has grown into a monster of deceit and greed, eroding the credibility of government and subverting the rule of law'.

Indeed, the number of deaths caused by smoking is in dispute. Causes of death may be open to interpretation. Number-crunching computers will select a variety of descriptions from death certificates and ascribe them to smoking. It could be that far fewer people die from smoking-related diseases than the official figures pumped out by governments, with deaths caused instead by stress, hereditary conditions, and other complications being lumped in with smokers' deaths. There's even a theory that 'fear kills' and that the more people hear about the hazards of smoking the more likely they are to die. Alternatively, there is a 'worst-case' scenario that all the concerns over smoking and passive smoking have a base in fact and that many deaths caused by smoking are going unrecognized.

What is certain is that both camps tend to cherry-pick statistics to fit their agendas. Likewise, they are keen to debunk theories that don't fit in with their own.

The statistical comparisons and the arguments they cause will continue to rage for years to come. It is worth pointing out that any study worth its salt takes into account elements like chance, coincidence, bias, corroborative evidence, plausibility, relative risk, risk factors, statistical significance, and cause and effect. Hypothetical risk versus sound scientific analysis will nevertheless remain a crucial field of battle and few issues outside smoking have as many research documents to their name. But there are some crimes of which smoking is guilty beyond reasonable doubt.

Smoking makes the heart work harder. As carbon monoxide replaces oxygen the heart must go faster to achieve the necessary oxygen levels for the body to work well. In addition, there is an associated build-up of deposits that clog blood vessels and arteries. In the process of smoking the heart muscles may be injured. For these reasons smoking is a cause of heart disease. One primary smokers' complaint is chronic-obstructive-pulmonary disease. A woman dying from it was described by her daughter: 'She will be 55 in March, is on oxygen 24 hours a day, lives on antibiotics, and can't even walk to the bathroom without struggling for breath.'

Cigarette smoke makes the natural cleaning process that takes place in the lungs much harder to achieve. Smoking gives voice to this otherwise largely silent cleaning process, hence 'the smoker's cough'.

Few smokers escape without suffering a smoker's cough at least some time in their lives, with morning time being a particular weak spot. Barking and abrasively distinct from all other coughs, it is an exhausting and unpleasant affliction.

No one describes the syndrome of the smoker's morning cough better than Spike Milligan (1918-2002), the father of alternative British comedy. In his memoirs of the Second World War *Adolf Hitler: My Part In His Downfall*, he devotes no fewer than 450 words to one hilarious description of the cough: 'The cough would start in silence...the victim started what was to be an agonized body spasm...the legs would bend, the hand grabbed the thighs to support the coming convulsion...from afar comes a rumbling like a hundred early-Victorian water closets...a sound like a three-ton garden roller being pulled over corrugated iron was heard approaching the heaving chest...the mouth would finally explode open! Loose teeth would fly out, bits of breakfast, and a terrible rasping noise filled the room... Finally, with a dying attempt, fresh air was sucked back into the body, just in time to do it all over again.'

Milligan, like most other soldiers, smoked during his years of army service but became strictly anti-smoking during his later years and plastered his home with signs to that effect.

The smoker's cough is but a trifle compared to the other lung diseases to which smokers are prone. Let's consider first the content of cigarette smoke. The smoke entering the lungs contains over 4,000 chemicals, including known cancer promoters. Among the worst culprits are tar (which stains the fingers and teeth), formaldehyde (used to preserve dead bodies), lead (so toxic it has been banned from paint), arsenic (widely administered by Victorian murderers), cadmium (used in batteries), acetone (the solvent in nail polish remover), ethanol (in antifreeze), ammonia (a cleaning agent), sulphuric acid (in the power station emissions that cause acid rain), and benzopyrene (one of the prime suspects in causing tumours).

> During the 20th century, smoking killed about 100 million people worldwide.

As mucus builds up in the lungs, particles from cigarette smoke can lodge in them and from there develop into tumours. What happens is that the compounds in the smoke act on the DNA of cells in the lungs, changing their behaviour. Most cells will not multiply unless there is a sound biological reason for them to do so. When healthy cells do divide and multiply the body will send out an order for the replication to halt. Cells that are altered by the carcinogenic ingredients in cigarette smoke will multiply for no reason and won't stop. This effect does not occur immediately and cells undergo a process before becoming cancerous. Smoking is the cause of most lung cancer cases worldwide. Only about ten per cent of lung cancer cases are attributable to something other than tobacco, for example, asbestos, environmental pollution and poor diet.

As far as lung cancer is concerned, the survival rates are woefully low. In America about 14 per cent of patients survive for five years and this is matched in some European countries. In the UK the figure is only five per cent. On average, the time lapse between diagnosis and death is four months. The prognosis has not substantially changed in Britain in 50 years. The symptoms of lung cancer include repeated chest infections, weight loss, tiredness, excess phlegm, spit coloured with blood, voice loss without a sore throat, chest pains, and facial and neck swellings. Victims take on a sagging, skeletal appearance.

Chewing tobacco can also cause cancer of the mouth and throat while cigar smokers are twice as likely as non-smokers to die from these kinds of oral diseases.

Smoke also irritates the bronchial tubes in the lungs and produces more mucus, making it harder to breathe and difficult to stop coughing. Lung damage sustained through smoking causes emphysema, also known as 'lung rot'. Nearly all cases of emphysema are sparked by long-term smoking. Anyone who smokes about 20 cigarettes a day will, sooner or later, probably have some sign of the disease. Recovery times from any lung diseases are slower among smokers.

Here is a selection of bite-sized chunks of health information widely acknowledged as fact – although some in the pro-smoking lobby will take issue even with the minutiae of accepted medical research.

Middle-aged men who smoke an average of 15 cigarettes a day are three times more likely to have a heart attack than their non-smoking friends. Smokers face a 50 per cent higher risk of having a stroke than non-smokers while anyone smoking more than 25 cigarettes a day has the highest chance of suffering a stroke.

Women smokers who take the contraceptive pill are ten times more likely to suffer heart attacks, strokes or arterial disease than non-smokers on the same pill. Smoking may impair fertility among women and can induce impotence among men. Pregnant women who smoke are likely to give birth to smaller babies because the tobacco smoke reduces the flow of blood in the placenta. The children of smokers run an increased risk of having asthma. Smokers suffer shortness of breath almost three times more often than non-smokers. This means their athletic performances are inhibited.

Smoking also exacerbates other complaints, as Dr Sara Murray Jordan explains: 'Nobody should smoke cigarettes – and smoking with an ulcer is like pouring gasoline on a burning house.'

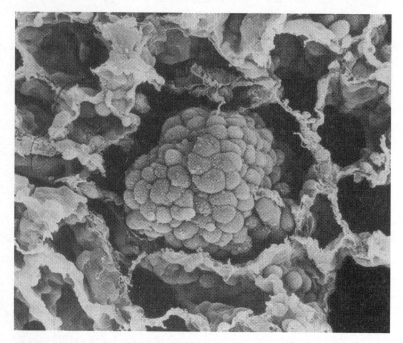

SEM (Scanning Electron Micrograph) shot of a small cancerous tumour filling an alveolus of the human lung. (Alveoli are the blind-ended air sacs that make up the lungs.) Here, the individual cancer cells are coated with microscopic, hair-like structures called microvilli. A number of cancer cells can also be seen separated from the main tumour.

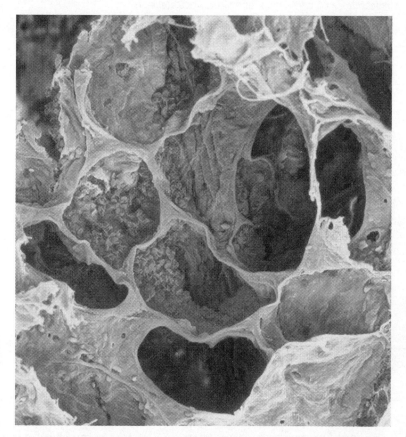

SEM shot of the haemorrhaging lung of a cancer sufferer, showing the thin-walled alveoli containing the red blood cells. This blood has haemorrhaged from the walls of the air sacs due to damage caused by the cancer. The patient was a heavy smoker and the affected lung had to be surgically removed.

For all of these reasons cigarettes have earned for themselves the nicknames of 'coffin nails' and 'little white slavers'.

Although few people these days deny that there are health risks attached to smoking, there are some outstanding exceptions to the rule. Everyone knows someone who smoked throughout a pregnancy and produced a bouncing, bigger-than-average baby. Hal Roach, director of numerous Laurel and Hardy film classics, lived for more than a century despite being a heavy smoker. Actor George Burns, invariably photographed with cigar in hand, died in 1996 at the age of 100. When Jeanne Louise Calment, of Arles, France, was lauded as the world's oldest woman (with birth certification), she made no secret of her smoking habit. When she died, in 1997, she was 122 years old. A Lebanese man claiming to be 134 years old was pictured on television smoking a cigarette. Some centenarians even put down their longevity to that fact that they smoke.

Likewise, there are tragic examples of men and women being struck down by lung cancer in their middle years having never smoked a cigarette in their lives. But to make a decision about whether or not to smoke based on this kind of anecdotal evidence is ludicrous in an era awash with information on the dangers of smoking.

However, it is also only fair to point out that stories about smokers going colour-blind, bald, sterile, and becoming sexually promiscuous were the stuff of fairy tales once put about in America to dissuade people from smoking. And the rumour that cigarette papers were saturated in arsenic persisted for many years but is likely to have grown out of a corruption of the facts.

One of the hot issues about smoking remains that of passive smoking, known as Environmental Tobacco Smoke, or ETS. Are smokers infecting those around them who are forced to breathe in tobacco fumes with lung cancer and heart disease? Concern about the effect of other people's smoke emerged at the end of the 1970s with demands that smoke should be kept out of the workplace. For the first time smoking rooms or areas were provided so that the air remained clean at least in places. Employers were reluctant to go further with an outright ban on smoking for fear of provoking a furore over personal rights and freedom of choice.

Within a decade, the bandwagon was rolling. At last those who hated the smell of cigarette smoke had legitimate reason to object. It has proved one of the most bitter and controversial arguments in the smoking debate, with each side furiously accusing the other of deceit and half-truths.

Let's take a quick tour of the argument that says passive smoking is bad for you. Tobacco smoke is one of a host of indoor pollutants ranging from gases emitted by cooking or heating appliances, mould spores, dust, and animal hairs. The most complex of these is, however, tobacco smoke, full to the brim with chemical compounds.

The effect of passive smoking is an increase in the heart rate and a decrease in oxygen supply. The blood vessels constrict and the heart must work harder. As far as effects on the body go, they are very much the same for smokers as for non-smokers.

There has been a clutch of studies on this very subject that has proved non-smokers are at risk from second-hand smoke. At its simplest level, smoke aggravates asthma and allergies. In addition, there is a whole range of other – often disputed – claims of its dangers.

In 1992 the US Environmental Protection Agency said that non-smoking women married to smokers were 19 per cent more likely to contract lung cancer than the rest of the population. In Britain a team from the Royal London School of Medicine found that non-smokers in smoking households faced an increased risk factor of between 26 per cent and 30 per cent.

The effect of smoking on babies and children is one of the most emotional subjects in the arena. As long ago as 1927 doctors in America were claiming that 60 per cent of infant deaths were due to the mother smoking. The infant mortality rate was, of course, much higher then than it is now. The ramifications of this shock statistic for a bereft mother were enormous. Many lived the rest of their lives in guilt and were even driven to suicide.

The issue of maternal smoking has ricocheted around in subsequent decades. For example, headlines in 1999 put the blame for cot deaths squarely on the shoulders of smoking parents. (Cot death, or SIDS [Sudden Infant Death Syndrome], is the sudden and unexpected death of a baby for no obvious reason.)

One study indicated that the rate of cot deaths among non-smoking households was about one in 5,000 while in homes where one or more people indulged the odds shortened to as little as one in 700. The greater the number of hours babies were exposed to second-hand smoke, the higher the risk. In addition, the effects of smoking were said to be increasing chest and ear infections and heightening the effects of childhood asthma.

Defenders of smokers and smoking have a different view. Flawed advice from the medical establishment was the cause of numerous cot deaths, they claim. For years it became standard to place a baby on its stomach to sleep. Then research indicated it was the prone position that posed a threat to sleeping babies. The number of cot deaths has been cut by about 70 per cent since 1991 when a 'Reduce the Risk of Cot Death' campaign was introduced.

This is correct, as far as it goes. Yes, putting babies to sleep on their backs instead of their fronts was a major thrust of the 1991 initiative. But the campaign also flagged up the dangers of smoking and included advice to mothers about avoiding smoking during pregnancy and afterwards. This, too, must have contributed to the dramatic decline. As Sarah Kenyon from the Foundation for the Study of Infant Deaths points out, no one yet knows the precise cause of cot deaths.

'About 40 per cent of America's 50 million smokers will try to kick the habit at least once this year. Fewer than one in ten will succeed.' Center for Disease Control and Prevention

But the research that has successfully highlighted ways of cutting the risk of cot deaths has been toying with the following statistics.

When mothers smoke during pregnancy their babies are up to 15 times more likely to die from cot death than the babies of non-smoking mothers. The risk of cot death increases according to the number of cigarettes women smoke per day while pregnant. Those who smoke up to nine cigarettes a day increase the risk to their babies five-fold. When more than 20 cigarettes are smoked each day, the risk is eight and a half times greater. If both parents smoke following the birth, the risk is eight times higher than that in a non-smoking household. If only the father smokes, the risk runs at three and a half times.

In the UK's largest ever cot-death study babies who died were at least twice as likely to have been exposed to tobacco smoke. So it seems that, post-natally, the more hours that babies are subjected to cigarette smoke, the greater the risk of cot death. One alarming facet of this debate is that a 1998 Department of Health survey revealed that only nine per cent of pregnant women knew that smoking during pregnancy increased the risk of cot death.

Of the nine steps young parents are urged to take to reduce the risk of cot death, two involve smoking less: that mothers and fathers cut out smoking during pregnancy and that no one should be permitted to smoke in the same room as the baby. The other seven steps are to place the baby on its back to sleep, not to let the baby get too hot, to keep the head uncovered, to seek medical advice if the baby is unwell, not to sleep in the same bed as the baby, to keep the cot in the parental bedroom for the first six months, and to avoid falling asleep on the sofa with the baby.

Despite these guidelines, seven babies still die every week in Britain through cot death and it remains the biggest killer of babies over one month old.

There's speculation that the effects of a smoking mother can be witnessed in her grandchildren. Linda Blanchard, the non-smoking daughter of two keen smokers, is certain it had an effect on her two children: 'My babies were both small. I often wondered if my mum smoking during pregnancy, when my own eggs were formed, made a difference.'

There's no doubt that the issue of passive smoking, even when babies and children are not at risk, unleashes strong emotions.

One report came to the frightening conclusion that, while only three in ten people believed they had been exposed to second-hand smoke during a test period, nine out of ten had detectable levels of smoke products in their bodies. Another said that a non-smoker in a smoke-laden room was inhaling the same as someone smoking 35 cigarettes every hour. One of the main areas of concern is the number of non-smokers in the hospitality industry, such as bar staff, who are exposed daily to high densities of second-hand smoke in the course of their working life.

In 2002 the London Assembly's Smoking in Public Places Committee called on the government to finance further investigations into passive smoking. Chair Jennette Arnold said, 'There is inadequate understanding of the links to heart disease and a clear need to raise public awareness of the health risks of passive smoking. In particular we need to make smokers more aware of the effects their smoke can have on non-smokers in the vicinity.'

Perhaps the most doom-laden report appeared in 2002 when research from Japan indicated that just 30 minutes in the company of a chain-smoker was enough to cause lung damage in a non-smoker. The pivotal point of the research was the response of special cells lining the cavities of the heart and blood vessels, whose purpose it is to stop clogging and clotting, during just 30 minutes of exposure to smoke.

An ultrasound measuring device discovered no change in the special cells of 15 smokers but the same number of non-smokers registered a change in their efficiency. The study appeared to prove that tobacco smoke had an impact on the heart of everyone who came into contact with it.

If an industrial pipe leaked damaging smoke it would be shut down, claimed anti-smoking campaigners. Yet passive smoking has been pretty well passively accepted despite the apparent hazards.

In America the Environmental Protection Agency issued a report in 1993 that branded second-hand smoke a 'Class A carcinogen' which killed as many as 3,000 non-smokers a year. It insists there is no safe level of exposure. Other people's cigarette smoke should be ranked on a par with asbestos and arsenic, the report insisted. The tobacco companies immediately charged the government with exaggeration but the official American line has stayed firm. Two thirds of the smoke from a burning cigarette is not inhaled but enters the surrounding environment. According to the US Department of Health and Human Services report on carcinogens this smoke is said to contain twice as much nicotine and tar as the smoke inhaled by smokers and five times the level of carbon monoxide.

Many doctors believe that inhaling second-hand smoke is the same as smoking. The strength of conviction of its harmful effects is such that Justice Robert F Julian, in the New York Supreme Court, prohibited a mother from smoking in the presence of her 13-year-old son because of the detrimental effects of second-hand smoke.

In 1992 British entertainer Roy Castle was diagnosed with lung cancer. Although the singer, dancer, and musician had never once sucked on a cigarette, he is thought to have contracted the disease by breathing in other people's smoke in pubs and clubs during his long career. Before his death he worked tirelessly to raise the profile of lung disease. His work was posthumously recognized when the Roy Castle International Centre for Lung Cancer Research was officially opened in Liverpool on 12 May 1998. It is the only research centre in the world solely dedicated to defeating lung cancer and works in conjunction with the University of Liverpool on research projects.

Pipe smoke is as toxic as cigarette smoke but cigar smoke is worse. One 5" (12.7cm) long cigar, the width of a human thumb, produces 30 times as much carbon monoxide as a cigarette, making a room hazardous to non-smokers within 30 minutes.

But wait, just when you were convinced that passive smoking would do for you, another side to this story is revealed. Scientists at Colorado State University looked again at the analysis which had thrown up the 25-per-cent lung cancer risk to non-smokers. The maths was mistaken, they claimed, and the threat posed by other people's cigarette smoke was in fact negligible.

In 1996 the European Working Group on Environmental Tobacco Smoke and Lung Cancer, made up from six scientists, investigated all 48 reports on passive smoking available to them at the time. Their view was that 'environmental tobacco smoke is not a primary lung carcinogen'.

A delay in the publication of a major investigation by the World Health Organization excited the pro-smoking lobbies. The report proved, they said, that anyone living with a smoker was not at risk from ETS, indeed, they could even benefit from a protective effect against lung cancer. The WHO claimed the findings were taken out of context but the happy smokers would hear none of it.

A spokesman for British American Tobacco conceded that science could not definitively prove that there was no risk associated with passive smoking. But he added, 'The studies on lung cancer to date, however, do not demonstrate that ETS is a cause of lung cancer and to the extent that these studies are used to suggest that there is a risk of lung cancer from ETS exposure, it is too small to measure with any certainty.

'Analysis of the data from the American Cancer Society's Cancer Prevention Study and the US National Mortality Followback Survey found no overall association between ETS and heart disease,' the spokesman continued. But he prudently fell back on common sense when it came to passive smoking and children.

'Quite a large number of studies report a statistically significant increase in respiratory symptoms in pre-school children exposed to ETS at home. Other studies have suggested a relationship between parental smoking and sudden infant death syndrome. Whether or not passive smoking plays a causal role in this, we believe it makes sense not to smoke around infants and young children, especially in poorly ventilated environments.'

There was a suspicion among smokers that the passive smoking controversy was pumped up by people who simply hated the smell of cigarettes. Cigarettes were smelly but so were people who ate garlic, didn't use deodorant, favoured cheap aftershave and hair oil or drank beer at lunchtime. Should these people also be restrained by law? Could the measures taken against smoking merely be political correctness gone mad? The ardent smoker who feels the dangers of passive smoking are as real as Nessie the Loch Ness Monster remains aghast at the amount of time and money wasted on whimsical notions.

Tobacco companies are always keen to emphasize the erosion of personal liberty. An editorial in *Tobacco International* reported, 'Communism is about the absence of choice, which is why it failed; smoking is about the freedom of choice, which is why it survives.'

A further factor is the extent to which pollution from cars, lorries and factories cause lung cancer and heart disease. American scientists have concluded that these factors are every bit as injurious to health as passive smoking.

More theories about smoking and health are springing up all the time. Among the latest to be circulated are the fact that smokers who eat two servings of cruciferous vegetables, such as cabbage and broccoli, each week have lower levels of tobacco-related toxins in their urine. This is according to the American Health Foundation and complements long-standing advice to eat fresh fruit and vegetables daily to avoid cancer. Scientists are looking at whether or not a drug used to cure a dry mouth also slows growth in pre-cancerous abnormalities in the airways of smokers and former smokers. A study by Danish and Japanese researchers suggests that couples who smoke after making love may be reducing their chances of having a son. The theory is that sperm carrying the male sex chromosome are more vulnerable to toxic chemicals in tobacco smoke and get killed off during the post coital cigarette. Sperm carrying the female chromosome are more durable. A British hospital is investigating a potential link between smoking and the onset of breast and bowel cancer.

'Smoking is one of the leading causes of statistics.' Author Fletcher Knebel

Quitting cigarettes has been a long-time cause of heartache and soul searching. Essayist and children's writer Charles Lamb (1775–1834) was addicted to tobacco and perpetually struggled to give it up. In a letter to Thomas Manning written just after Christmas in 1815 he wrote, 'This very night I am going to leave off tobacco! Surely there must be some other world in which this unconquerable purpose shall be realized. The soul hath not her generous aspirings implanted in her in vain.' Clearly, he had formed certain opinions about the damage tobacco was doing to him. In his work *A Farewell To Tobacco* he wrote, 'For thy sake, Tobacco, I would do anything but die.'

It may seem like an impossible dream to wannabe non-smokers but it is possible to kick the habit. One of the most recent success stories is Camilla Parker-Bowles, Prince Charles's companion, a smoker for some 39 years before she stopped as part of a New Year's Resolution. Nicotine patches helped reduce her craving for cigarettes. After three months the Prince – a fervent anti-smoker like his mother and grandmother – was said to be delighted. One cigarette puffed at the age of 11 was sufficient to put him off for life. The Queen's father and sister were heavy smokers and both died prematurely.

Some people insist that giving up cigarettes is the hardest thing they have ever done. Express even a tiny bit of interest and you will be regaled by stories of temptation, misery, cravings, and crises. They want praise for achieving their goal in the face of monstrous adversity – and why not? Giving up smoking takes some guts.

However, other ex-smokers adopt a less dramatic line. 'If people really want to do it, they will,' one told me. 'If they don't, they won't.'

There's another sizeable chunk of the smoking population who insists that giving up is 'mission impossible'. They are of the same school of thought as writer Mark Twain, who wrote, 'To cease smoking is the easiest thing I ever did. I ought to know, because I've done it 1,000 times.'

Millions try to give up smoking every year but only a few succeed. Some put the figure at ten per cent

> People who quit smoking immediately begin to reduce the risk of developing lung cancer, compared with those who still smoke. The risk levels among people who have given up smoking for more than ten years are in the same ball park as non-smokers.

still staying true to their resolution a year later, other research bodies feel the true figure is much lower. According to the Royal College of Physicians, 'Over two-thirds of smokers say they would like to quit and about one third try to quit in any year, yet only two per cent succeed.'

In reality, most smokers in the process of quitting feel frustrated, angry, anxious, hungry, restless and listless. They may have difficulty in concentrating for long periods or in sleeping. Some suffer mouth ulcers, a sore tongue, constipation and diarrhoea. Other symptoms of withdrawal include headaches and a decreased heart rate.

But the benefits can be felt surprisingly quickly. According to the Roy Castle International Centre for Lung Cancer Research the body begins to repair itself immediately. Within just 20 minutes blood pressure and pulse rate return to normal and circulation improves. Just eight hours after giving up the nicotine and carbon monoxide levels in the blood are slashed in half. Oxygen levels start to approach regular levels and so the threat of a heart attack recedes.

Those that manage 24 hours without a cigarette will no longer have a body tainted by carbon monoxide. In 48 hours the body is free of nicotine and you can anticipate the return of the senses of smell and taste.

Energy levels should be boosted after 72 hours of being smoke-free and you will be breathing more easily. Between three and nine months after stopping your lung function will have increased by up to ten per cent. After five years the risk of a heart attack has diminished to half that of a smoker. Ten years after stopping the risk of getting lung cancer is equal to half that facing a smoker while the probability of a heart attack is the same as that of a non-smoker.

There's no doubt that for the majority smokers it does take a phenomenal effort to escape the tyranny of nicotine although anyone who quits for more than a year has an 85 per cent chance of remaining smoke-free. But, as one journalist observed, 'There are two parts to quitting smoking. One is giving up cigarettes. This is actually a pretty simple thing to do. You just sit quietly in one place and breathe as deeply as you can. The second part of quitting smoking is living without cigarettes. This is extremely difficult.'

But the message from health authorities is, 'don't give up giving up'. As one American professor put it, 'Most people have to try to quit probably five to seven times before they succeed. It's just like swimming, it's important to keep jumping in the water to learn.'

There are more crutches than ever before to assist the quitter. Anyone with access to the Internet will find a bountiful number of sites offering help and advice for reluctant smokers. Britain's 'Quit', a national charity devoted to helping people succeed, is a prime example with its helpline service and bevy of counsellors. Quit has devoted an entire arm of its operations to aiding young people who started smoking early.

'Given that statistics in a recent survey carried out by ASH and No-Smoking Day showed that 83 per cent of smokers would not start if they had their time again, and reports stating that "most adult smokers do not smoke out of choice but because they become addicted to nicotine when they start smoking as adolescents", it is crucial that we raise awareness of this issue in the minds of young people,' said Alex Frost, of Quit.

Talks to adolescents must be pitched exactly right if they are to hit the mark. 'Our Break Free presentations are informative but not patronising and empower the young people to make their own decision about smoking,' Frost explained.

'Young people tend to be fairly well educated in the health problems which smoking can contribute to, for example, cancers and heart disease. However, we also raise awareness of less well-known health effects, for example, amputations caused by blood clots. Also the chemicals the body is exposed to through smoking – including arsenic, carbon monoxide, nicotine, tar, acetone, formaldehyde and ammonia.

'There's the financial implications of smoking. The average smoker on ten-a-day will spend nearly £750 ($1,100) in a year, enough to buy around 60 CDs, a designer suit or a holiday in Ibiza.

'And we highlight methods used by the tobacco industry to raise awareness of their products, like sponsorship of motor racing and product placement in films.

'The chief aim of the presentations is to provide young people with the facts, encourage them to question what smoking means to them and ask themselves, "Is smoking worth it?" '

Film director and newspaper columnist Michael Winner now believes smoking isn't worth the high price many smokers pay. Winner, best remembered for the *Death Wish* movie starring Charles Bronson, was a cigar smoker who puffed his way through 15 large Havanas a day. 'By the end of the day my heart was pumping at unnatural speed. My mouth was dry. I could hardly talk. My breathing was laboured. Everyone around me smelt of cigar smoke.'

In 1993 he landed in intensive care needing open-heart surgery. The trauma stopped his smoking habit although he still believes that 40 years of indulgence will probably knock ten years off his life.

Shock tactics also worked for one 60-year-old, Ron Waters, who, living in London's suburbs, saw his neighbour die of a heart attack. He even tried to resuscitate him before he breathed his last. Ron accompanied the widow to the hospital, to be told that the dead man would have lived longer if only he hadn't smoked. On that day he gave up his 40-a-day habit which had prevailed for some 45 years with an ease that surprised friends and family – although 20 years later he can still be seen patting his pockets from shoulders to hips to locate the packets of cigarettes which were once his constant companions.

Adam Hamilton has embarked on yet another attempt to give up cigarettes. 'The decision was taken entirely on health grounds – I do miss the old friend and have deliberately not gone around boasting about how I've "given up". I've given up several times in the past – the longest I lasted was a year. My mum always worried about me smoking, to the extent that lung cancer had become our main topic of conversation. She was so relieved when she heard I'd given up years ago that I didn't have the heart

> Half of all smoking-related deaths occur between the ages of 35 and 69, which translates into an average of roughly 23 years of life lost.

to tell her I'd relapsed. She made it easy by always asking leading questions that presumed I'd still given up – so I only had to go along with it. I always saw it as a "white lie", told so as not to cause her unnecessary worry, though I was aware that it somehow embodied the immaturity of my relationship with her.

'It often occurred to me that she knew I still sometimes smoked – she'd often comment on the smell on my clothes, though usually prefacing it with some explanation that offered me a way out. The catch 22 was that the more she let me know how much she worried about smoking, the more I'd divert my own anxiety about the health risks into worrying about upsetting her – and the more I could do with a ciggy.

'I've now decided not to smoke for the foreseeable future and already feel much better for it. I think of it not so much as giving up smoking as taking up breathing.

'In the end it's a habit, an addiction, and once an addict [always an addict]. As with all junk, when you kick the habit you're left with a hole in your life, which renders you always susceptible. Tobacco is not as addictive as smack but a lot more habit forming than, say, cannabis. The trouble is, having smoked joints since I was about 17, I'd become dependent on the mixture and particularly addicted to the tobacco in a joint. In the past whenever I've given up "straight" cigarettes I've tended to compensate by smoking loads of joints.'

Kim Jones, a college lecturer, witnessed first-hand the misery caused by one woman's fight to quit cigarettes.

'I had an aunt who died of lung cancer in her early 50s after making many attempts to give up. She was a nurse who smoked 60 a day. Her consultant told her it would be better if she got a really fast car for an alternative adrenalin buzz, or a toy boy. He said even heroin would be better for her than cigarettes. She was so shocked by what she heard she had to go outside to have a cigarette.

'She was a Catholic and she would ring her priest in desperation in the middle of the night when she was trying to give up. This was an intelligent woman who understood what smoking was doing to her but couldn't do anything about it.'

At work in a further education college, Jones remains concerned about smoking levels today. 'I hate it because smoking is seen as "cool" when really it is scary. In September and October I see many young people trying to look cool with a cigarette. To them it is a fashion accessory and it stops you eating. That is a double bonus as far as they are concerned. I often nag the students here about smoking. They look at me as though I'm mad.'

Administrator Terry Walmsley, 48, stopped a 30-a-day habit on the advice of his doctor after suffering high blood pressure. Within months he was stricken with heart trouble and believes he abandoned smoking in the nick of time.

'I gave up at Christmas after 30 years of smoking. I didn't bother with any patches. I was very short tempered and my sleep pattern was affected so I was waking up during the night. I was in a state for a while. But I got a lot of support from my wife.'

It was not the first time he had quit. 'When I was in my 20s I gave up for 18 months but I never lost the urge for a cigarette. I was living with a mother who smoked and two brothers who smoked. Eventually I succumbed.'

For years Walmsley convinced himself that he would give up 'one day'. 'Like everyone else I saw these people on the television who were about to die of smoking-related diseases – and they still wanted a cigarette. It is so easy to think, "That is someone else," but it will be you, 10, 15 or 20 years down the line.'

He admits that, immediately after quitting, it would not have taken much for him to start smoking again even after having received a tough talking-to from his doctor. 'It takes a lifestyle change to succeed. For a while I stopped going down the pub. About ten days after I gave up I went in and had a pint. The bloke next to me lit up so I just knocked back my drink and left. I knew if I was to hang about I would have had one. Months later I still find it difficult but not as much.'

Despite the personal hardships it has brought him, Walmsley has no difficulty with tobacco companies. 'Cigarette companies didn't force me to buy cigarettes or to smoke them. I did it myself. I used to love smoking. Sometimes especially under stress I could come out of my office and get outside, light up a cigarette and everything seemed better. If I had a problem, I would think, "I will go and have a smoke and think about this." But maybe I reached a time in my life when it wasn't right for me any more.'

A 55-year-old man relates his story of being fume-free. 'I started at the age of 12 because everyone at school smoked. It was just something you did back then and no one ever mentioned the health risks. I finally managed to give up when the doctor told me I had a lung problem and it was essential to stop immediately. It wasn't as hard as I had anticipated. At first it used to drive me crazy for a cigarette, if people blew smoke in my face. Now I just find it disgusting. A lot of older people I know are giving up for health reasons and are trying to forbid their younger offspring from taking up smoking. It doesn't work, though, and there seem to be a lot of young people who smoke heavily these days. Far more than us older ones.'

Although only a social smoker June Aiken gave up cigarettes after 22 years of smoking. 'For years I kidded myself I could stop if I wanted to. I never really tried because deep down I was worried about failing. When I finally made up my mind to do it, I got the shakes and that skin-creeping sensation. I was very aware that my nerves were jangling. I felt I needed a cigarette. One cigarette and I knew I would feel fine again. Fortunately I resisted. I still quite like the smell when someone lights up and the smoke isn't too dense. It's very evocative for me. But I won't smoke again.'

Joseph Lowe, from Florida, quit after 38 years of smoking. He grew up in a household of smokers – his mother ultimately died of lung cancer and his father heart disease. 'All those years I was smoking second-hand smoke and didn't know it. I believe I was addicted before I even started smoking.' Although he disliked the smell of the family home, Lowe's friends persuaded him to smoke. 'We all wanted to be the "Marlboro Man". It was cool to smoke. You weren't a man if you didn't smoke and a wuss if you didn't inhale.'

Finally, a smoker's cough and pressure from his asthmatic sons forced him to quit, which proved to be something of a mountain to climb. 'Cigarettes were my best friend. They were always there when I needed them – when I was sad, hurting, no matter what the situation – and they didn't criticize me.' He's gained weight and stopped socializing with smokers. But despite feeling the occasional urge for a cigarette, Lowe has managed to remain fume-free.

Cravings appear to be reduced by nicotine replacement, which can be delivered by patches, gum, inhalers and nasal sprays. The treatments introduce limited and declining quantities of nicotine to the system while being free of the harmful elements of cigarette smoke. The body isn't suddenly bereft of nicotine and the quitter can concentrate on finding new rituals for his hands before conquering the bodily desires. Britons trying to give up cigarettes spend in excess of £32 million ($46.75 million) on tobacco substitutes each year.

However, there's a temptation to under-dose oneself in order to save money and that points to the path of failure. Anyone who believes that patches, first introduced in 1992, and other replacement therapies are like a magic pill to quell all desire for cigarettes are also in for a sad awakening. By comparison to the simple cigarette, patches, gum and the rest are by no means completely satisfactory.

'The unique selling point of tobacco is its nicotine content – tobacco products without nicotine are not commercially viable,' says the Royal College of Physicians. 'Nicotine is an addictive drug and the primary purpose of smoking tobacco is to deliver a dose of nicotine rapidly to receptors in the brain. This generates a pleasurable sensation for the smoke which, with repeated experience, rapidly consolidates into physiological and psychological addiction reinforced by pronounced withdrawal symptoms.

'The speed of nicotine delivery is a fundamental difference between cigarettes and nicotine replacement therapy products which deliver nicotine at lower and slower sub-addictive rates.'

Being hooked on tobacco is a complicated issue, as we've seen, and giving up is not just about being deprived of nicotine. It is also about being disarmed in social or work situations. Abstain from smoking and an entire lifestyle can unravel before your eyes.

A second load of nicotine-infused goodies appeared on shop shelves in America in 2002. Concern was quickly raised about the sale of lollipops laced with nicotine, which on the face of it might help a quitting smoker but in fact might hook a child on the habit. There was even a fear the amount of nicotine inside the candy-type product would be physically harmful to children.

Nicotine lollies, lip balm and tobacco lozenges were soon marketed over the Internet and were readily available to computer-literate youngsters. Initially the goods appeared to fall outside the remit of America's powerful Food and Drug Administration, which advises on public health and safety. But an investigation found that the nicotine used in the lollipops was made from a different form to that in the more recognizable gum and patches and had not undergone the necessary safety checks. It meant the FDA could ban the sale of lollipops and lip balm, which it duly did in April 2002, and take a closer look at lozenges. Larry Melton, the owner of the pharmacy where the lollies were created, said he had been responding to a demand from customers for alternatives to gum and patches.

In Britain cigarettes and associated products are exempt from most forms of consumer protection. As the Royal College of Physicians explains, 'This anachronistic situation has arisen, first, because cigarettes were already on the market when consumer protection laws were being developed and, secondly, because the extent of the harm caused by cigarettes to the consumer is such that they do not and – without radical changes probably cannot – meet the safety requirements imposed on other products.'

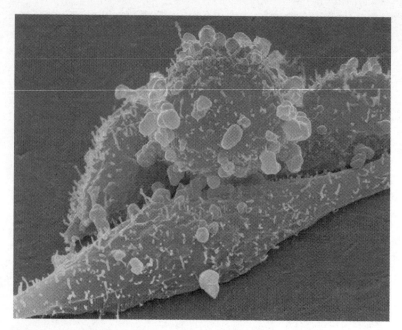

SEM shot of lung-cancer cells.

Light micrograph of human lung tissue showing a branch of the pulmonary artery blocked by an embolus originating from a clot in the deep veins of the leg. Fragments of thrombus may become detached from their site of formation and travel in the circulation as thromboemboli. On reaching vessels small enough to prevent further passage, the thromboemboli become lodged and cause obstruction to blood flow. Depending on the degree of obstruction and extent of alternative blood supply, the result is either a reduced blood supply to the tissue (ischaemia) or its total cessation, leading to tissue death.

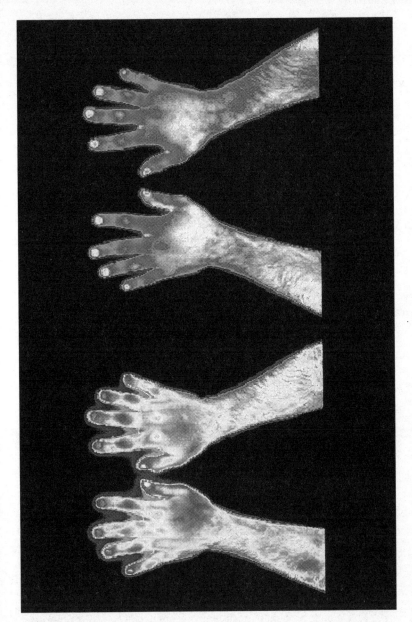

Thermogram of forearms seen before (LEFT) and five minutes after (RIGHT) smoking a cigarette, show the skin's temperature by displaying its emission of infrared radiation. Here, the temperature scale runs from over 34° Celcius through 33°, 32°, and 30–1° to 28–9°. After smoking, the blood vessels have undergone vasoconstriction (narrowing), cooling the forearms by reducing the amount of blood flowing into them. The narrowing is mainly due to nicotine.

Doctors and nurses are coached in helping patients to give up smoking while they are in hospital. Curiously, nicotine replacement therapy, the most likely route for most people who want to quit, has not until recently been freely available in Britain when those addicted to illicit drugs and alcohol were helped without charge. One health-care professional in America remains perplexed by a similar situation in the States. 'It is important that smokers, doctors, insurers and the US Congress hear what a paradox it is that our health system spends tens of billion of dollars to provide care for heart attacks or strokes or lung cancer or emphysema but it does not pay for medicine that could help people quit smoking.'

The decision to provide help for would-be quitters in Britain grew out of controversy. The nicotine-free anti-smoking drug Zyban was at the centre of a row following the death of 21-year-old air hostess Kerry Weston, of Hertfordshire, England. She died after taking Zyban for two weeks, alongside an anti-malarial drug and insomnia tablets. A coroner who investigated the case ruled that the drug played a part in her death. In Britain its opponents linked it to 58 deaths and more than 7,000 side effects including stress, insomnia, rashes, headaches, nausea, vomiting, and depression.

Zyban works by suppressing the biochemical basis for nicotine addiction. After it was launched in Britain in 2000 as the country's first anti-smoking drug, it was available for only six months before Britain's medicines watchdog, the National Institute for Clinical Excellence (NICE), began an investigation into it and other treatments to help people stop smoking.

In April 2002 NICE published a report backing the use of Zyban. Further, it urged that Zyban and other nicotine replacement therapies should be available on prescription. The link between Zyban and the deaths of users remains unproven although the report recognized that it presented a greater risk to those who were diabetic or to anyone taking appetite suppressants. The risk of a seizure appears to run at about one in a thousand patients.

Appeasing the accountants who might have been concerned that potential quitters – a notoriously fickle bunch – would squander National Health Service resources in a 'will-I, won't-I?' programme of giving up, new rules have been brought in governing prescription of the drug. Smokers can only get help if they have set a date for quitting. In general Zyban is prescribed in a two-month course. If patients lapse they are not be permitted treatment for a further six months.

Anne-Toni Rodgers, the executive director of NICE, says, 'The guidance means that the NHS will be supporting smokers who are motivated to quit with a choice of clinically- and cost-effective treatments.'

Anti-smoking groups had been concerned that the risks presented by smoking were far higher than those of Zyban and that the benefits of quitting – and Zyban can double the chances of a cigarette smoker successfully giving up – were being lost in a smoke screen. Some of the side effects attributed to Zyban were probably caused by smoking or smoking cessation, they had insisted.

Sir Paul Nurse, joint director general of Cancer Research UK, confirmed that smoking cessation treatments were probably the most effective way of spending NHS money.

Another route for would-be quitters is hypnotherapy. But how does it work? The therapist reaches the unconscious mind and aims to change behaviour patterns that have become entrenched through years of smoking. Hypnotherapist Mark Warwick, of London, begins by talking to clients on the content of cigarette smoke, the cost of smoking and the hazards it presents. He is not only setting out his stall but is lulling people into a state of relaxation so the business of hypnotherapy can begin. Talking all the while in a monotone voice, the client will ultimately 'switch off'.

> 'Sweet, when the morn is grey; Sweet when they've cleared away Lunch; and at the close of day, Possibly sweetest.'
> 'Ode To Tobacco', Charles Stuart Calverley (1831–84)

Warwick explains his method: 'We "bore" the conscious mind to get through to the subconscious. For the client it is like being absorbed in a book. They are aware of what is going on around them but they're concentrating so much on the book they don't look up.'

There are a variety of techniques at his disposal. He believes one of the most effective is the Emotional Freedom Technique, which is achieved through acupuncture points and has come to Britain from the United States.

Whichever course he pursues, Warwick is hoping to lead his clients out of addiction. He will suggest an alternative use for idle hands or instill a negative response when a cigarette is offered. Sometimes clients leave his sessions with a violent dislike of cigarettes replacing a previous dependency. For others a ritual, like smoking with a cup of coffee, is broken.

Warwick believes that hypnotherapy is effective in at least eight out of ten cases but finds women more of a challenge than men. 'It is harder for females to give up smoking than males. I think it must be their hormones because many give up just like that during pregnancy, when their hormones are awry.'

Perhaps his biggest success story is persuading one 100-a-day smoker to quit. 'He ripped half the inside of his car out afterwards because he hated the smell so much,' Warwick recalls.

A single session, lasting no more than two hours, is usually sufficient to transform the lifelong habits of a smoker, Warwick insists. There are back-up sessions available to those who relapse. The cost often deters people but in Britain a session with Warwick is equivalent to about 25 packets of cigarettes, not bad value if the hypnotherapy is successful. 'You should save the money within a couple of weeks,' he promises.

'In 1998, the United States harvested 718,000 acres of tobacco producing 1.48lb billion (671kg million) of tobacco leaf. The 1998 crop had a value of $3.049 billion (£2.088 billion), with $1.46 billion (£716 million) worth of leaf being exported.' **Philip Morris**

People who choose to give up with the help of counselling or a support group are more likely to succeed than those who go-it-alone. Most western countries have telephone helplines readily available for anyone wishing to give up smoking.

For the lone quitter there are some standard pieces of advice in cutting down with a view to quitting. Try drawing a line a quarter of the way between the filter and the tip and stop smoking the cigarette when you reach the line. Gradually move the line towards the tip so that you smoke less and less each week. If you are a pack-a-day person discard two cigarettes each morning. That way you will end up smoking fewer, hopefully without breaking the habit of buying a single packet. Increase the number you discard in the weeks and months ahead. When you feel it is time to stop smoking, make a date to do so and stick with it.

Quitting smoking means retraining the brain. Remember, you will still feel the urge to smoke whether or not you light up each time. Likewise, the urge will gradually diminish whether you smoke or not.

Drink lots of water, as an oral alternative to cigarettes and to avoid gaining weight. Give yourself non-nicotine treats – as anyone who pursues a punishing course of deprivation will surely lapse unless they pamper themselves in other ways. Think positive! Don't think of yourself as a quitter, with all the negative connotations that the word brings. Instead, why not break free from smoking, release yourself, be motivated to stop? All these are happier ways of expressing your course of action. Breathe deeply. Enjoy the fresh air in a way your lungs would not let you do before giving up. Start to haunt non-smoking areas like churches, museums and theatres. Stay away from temptation.

Persuade a friend to give up with you. With access to mobile phones, text messaging, emails, and so forth you will be able to offer one another unprecedented levels of support.

Focus on the benefits of giving up smoking. Your blood pressure will return to normal levels, as will your heart rate. Your hands and feet will feel warmer – less remote – thanks to improved circulation. Phlegm production recedes and at the same time the senses of taste and smell will be boosted. You will feel more energetic and be able to exercise for longer. At last it's worth investing in some pricey aftershave or perfume as you will no longer be reeking of *eau d'ashtray*.

Sit in non-smoking areas whenever possible so that you are not allowed to light up. Keep a diary of how you think and feel to identify strategies for not smoking that work for you. Switch to another brand of cigarette so the flavour and sensation is alien. Hold your cigarette in the opposite hand to the one you normally use. This will take away some of the automatic behaviour that smokers suffer from.

Be prepared if you are going to give up. Arm yourself with chewing gum to keep your mouth occupied. Buy crayons and paper to keep your hands busy. Learn some relaxation techniques that you can practise anywhere,

Radio drive-time host Bill Mayhugh, from Washington, DC, feels the key to kicking the habit lies in the difference between knowing and believing that smoking is bad for you. 'To know is to have knowledge of something,' Bill says. 'To believe is to accept as fact that which you know.' This way smokers cross the bridge from knowing that smoking is a health hazard to accepting responsibility for the harm it does.

It is, however, impossible to know which is the best approach or the most successful therapy for each individual.

Allen Carr is the self-styled saviour of the smoker with an evangelical approach to quitting. After conquering a 100-a-day habit, he penned two books with the seductive titles *The Easy Way To Stop Smoking* and *The Only Way To Stop Smoking Permanently* which have been translated into 20 languages and have sold more than five million copies worldwide. An unknown number of people have been given second-hand copies by friends who have seen the light and want to spread the word.

Being a former smoker, Carr has more credibility than most. He had his first cigarette when he was about 11 years old – and it wasn't a pleasant experience: 'It was during the War and practically every male smoked then. It was a macho, tough-guy thing to do. Myself and two friends pooled our pocket money to buy five Woodbines. We smoked one each, which meant there were two left.

'I felt absolutely green, I just wanted to get away and be sick. The writing was on the wall when one of my friends said, "You two can have the couple that are left." That phrase was completely foreign to us. If it had been oranges or bananas we would have been fighting for them. Even then I thought, "How can anyone get hooked on these things?" '

Anyone who smokes more than 40 cigarettes a day increases the chance of dying by between 200 and 300 per cent, in comparison with non-smokers.

Disgusted by this first experience Carr stayed away from cigarettes until he was working as an audit clerk away from home. 'The man in charge of the audit was a chain smoker and all the time kept offering me cigarettes. In the end I sensed he needed someone to smoke with him. He was persistent and eventually I took one. It was almost as bad as the first one. But I went on accepting them, thinking I was doing him a favour. Then eventually one day he said it was time I bought a packet. I thought, "Pay money for this rubbish?" But I didn't want to appear mean so I did buy a packet to pay him back. Then suddenly when my packet had gone I thought I would like another packet. I was in the trap.'

As Carr points out, he can recall the occasion when he took his first cigarette but he cannot remember making a decision to smoke 100 cigarettes a day. What's more, the decision to stop smoking is inevitably postponed until tomorrow, next week or sometime in the future. 'A fly gets a whiff of the nectar in a pitcher plant and it has no choice but to answer that call. Smokers are not choosing to smoke, they are getting sucked along into a very clever, subtle confidence trick.

> 'The children of mothers who smoke during pregnancy are at increased risk of neonatal mortality or sudden-infant-death syndrome, of asthma and/or wheezing illness in the first years of life and they subsequently experience impaired physical growth and academic attainment compared to children of non-smoking mothers.' Royal College of Physicians

He likens smoking to any manner of addiction: 'No one needs cigarettes before they start smoking. They always taste awful to start with and you think, "There is nothing in this." Before you know it you think, "I'm enjoying this, I'm in control." You are not. If you are being fooled in a confidence trick you are not in control nor are you until you see through the confidence trick, then you don't fall for it anymore, you opt out.'

His view is backed up by the Royal College of Physicians who agree that 'addiction to tobacco products creates a demand for habitual use which is no longer an expression of consumer choice'.

Carr comes at smoking from a different angle to most counsellors: 'All the methods since the cancer scares of the '60s and before are based on saying that smoking is a stupid habit – which every smoker knows already. What my method does is to look at the other side of the tug of war, not that it is killing you, costing you a fortune, is filthy and disgusting but trying to assess what you are getting out of it. You didn't need cigarettes before you started smoking. The habit is just like banging your head against a brick wall so that you can get the pleasure of stopping.'

The desire for a cigarette occurs when the last vestiges of nicotine leave the body. Without the nicotine, the body experiences the flutter of panic. When the nicotine is replaced, people feel more confident – or less unrelaxed, at least. But of course smoking has little to do with logic, as Carr points out: 'Smokers say they like to smoke when they are bored and they like to smoke when they are concentrating. Boredom and concentration are complete opposites. Or they say they like to smoke when they are relaxing and they like to smoke in a stressful situation. Again, these are complete opposites.

> In 1996 more than 336,000 Australian schoolchildren smoked a total of more than 370 million cigarettes.

'If I tried to sell a magic pill that did the complete opposite of what it did an hour before you would know it wasn't possible and you would have me locked up as a charlatan. But that is what society and smokers themselves believe smoking does for them.'

He fervently believes that smoking is not about being strong-willed but about by-passing the brainwashing that has gone on in the mind of the smoker for years before: 'Most smokers believe they enjoy the taste and the smell of a cigarette. You don't have to smoke yourself to smell it, you can breathe in somebody else's. You may like the taste, but would you eat cigarettes? Smoking is like wearing tight shoes, just to get the relief of taking them off.

'It is a common misconception that chain smokers like myself are people who really enjoy smoking. I loathed it because I knew it was controlling me. When I found it wasn't a weakness in me and that there was nothing special in nicotine that I needed I was like the Count of Monte Cristo, suddenly finding I was free after spending years in prison. Over 18 years later I still can't get over the pleasure of being free.'

The key to stop young people smoking lies in education: 'If you could explain to a mouse how a mousetrap works and that if it touches that piece of cheese it will end up with an awful iron bar across it no mouse would ever be tempted into a trap again. No youngsters ever believe they will get hooked, because they don't understand the nature of the drug. We must explain how the trap works and that if they are tempted to take one cigarette they will have to take another and another and another.'

In addition to writing books, Allen Carr oversees a chain of clinics which operate in every continent except Antarctica. At these clinics the de-programming of smokers takes an estimated four hours. The key is to persuade people that they can cope and enjoy life without a cigarette.

One of the world's most unusual stories about giving up smoking belongs to Bob Friend, of Newbern, Tennessee. He made the mistake of blowing smoke gently in the face of Annie, his miniature American Eskimo dog. The dog responded by coughing and spluttering and clearly made a canine vow to cure Bob of his addiction.

Every time the dog heard the click of Bob's cigarette lighter she jumped on to his lap and repeated the wheezing noises. In the car she would place her face by the vent and appear to choke every time Bob lit up. Finally Bob got the message and gave up cigarettes, although it took him two attempts to do it. He admitted it wasn't easy, but having a smoking buddy like Annie kept his mind on the task and made it impossible to falter.

For those who find quitting impossible, the search for a nicotine vaccine continues. At the Minneapolis Medical Research Foundation, a vaccine has been developed that reduces by as much as 65 per cent the amount of nicotine passing from the blood to the brain in rats. It may be possible one day to have a jab that will reduce the thrill associated with smoking and so make it easier to quit.

One would-be quitter wrote this bleak message on www.quitnet.com: 'Well, I am back again. They say that the third time's a charm. Hope they are right. This is the third time this year that I am quitting. The last time I went back to smoking I got so depressed that I didn't want to talk to anyone for a long time. Can't say I will make it, can't say I won't. I'm just going to take this one minute, hour and day at a time.'

Once they have given up, reformed smokers often become vehemently opposed to the habit. Characteristically, they vilify cigarettes and those who smoke them with venom.

According to Tim Coulson, reformed smokers are the biggest thorn in the side of smokers: 'Reformed smokers with attitude would be the first with their back against the wall when the revolution comes. "I'd rather you didn't smoke in our garden. To be honest, we believe there should be a total ban." All this from somebody you last spoke to when they were a committed smoker.'

Says Jane Dennehy, 'There is the person who is always going to "give up tomorrow" and needs to learn that tomorrow never comes. If they ever get around to it they are going to be your typical, annoying reformed smoker who drives everyone mad with their puritan approach to life. Smokers, like alcoholics and other addicts, are addicted for life. Smokers who have "given up" have merely found other things to do to cover their dependence.'

Jane has no plans to give up smoking. 'I take smoking like I take life, one day at a time. I am always prepared, I always smoke my own brand, I don't offer cigarettes or accept them in return. I appreciate non-smokers' private space and would never smoke in someone's house unless invited to, and usually only if they smoke themselves.

'I don't talk about giving up because I think one day I will wake up and will have had enough. Until that happens I defend my right to have vices and habits and trust that I will continue to meet interesting people in the smokers anonymous section of events that I attend.'

So how does smoking rate alongside its twin vice, alcohol? A recent study by the American Council on Science and Health revealed that moderate consumption of alcoholic beverages can provide significant health benefits while no such benefits were ascribed to tobacco consumption. Lots of people knock back one or two drinks without exhibiting any harmful effects. Some research has found damage caused by smoke occurs within the first 30 minutes – although the problems that accrue through smoking can largely be undone through a period of abstinence.

05 MONEY

While smoking became a hobby-turned-Holocaust, the tobacco companies as its purveyors seemed in danger of becoming as outdated as Jurassic dinosaurs.

For a while there, old-established businesses that had enjoyed a secure niche in the international money market were assuming all the investment potential of a three-legged donkey running at the Kentucky Breeders' Cup. But tobacco companies responded to the challenge brought about by anti-smoking campaigns and legislation, exhibiting a refreshing resilience in an era that has seen the collapse of giants like Enron and Barings Bank. Profits are largely heading in the right direction and they have flourished, despite an uncertain stock market. It took a major commercial overhaul to bring the rabbit out of the hat.

Following a groundswell of opinion against smoking in the '70s and '80s, tobacco companies were forced to take a long, hard look at themselves. With one eye on the future, they no longer merely continued to give customers what they wanted, pretending that this was justification enough for their existence. Ultimately they chose to tackle head-on the newly installed moral issues surrounding their products, boldly pontificating on ticklish subjects like youth smoking rather than hiding from them with their heads in the sand. Following criticism surrounding corporate secrecy and duplicity, tobacco firms are now surprisingly transparent, and some companies have continued to diversify into other products. This may not satisfy everyone – some people maintain that cigarette manufacturers are peddling in grim addiction and death, using weasel words to defend the indefensible – but the forward-thinking business strategies have paid off as tobacco companies remain attractive business propositions.

To illustrate how times and attitudes have changed, check this out. In 1976 the Vice President of Philip Morris announced on TV that apple sauce was harmful to anyone who ate too much of it and went on to say, 'I think that if the company as a whole believed cigarettes were really harmful we would be out of business. We're a very moralistic company.' Everyone already knew that cigarettes were probably pretty dangerous and it is likely he knew that better than most. Can you imagine anyone saying that now?

In 1999, when asked by a House of Commons' Select Committee on Health whether smoking causes lung cancer, BAT, RJ Reynolds, and Philip Morris answered yes. Gallaher and Imperial were less unequivocal in their answers but Imperial conceded that smoking 'may be' a cause of disease while Gallaher said statistics meant it was 'more probable than not'. In addition, all the companies admitted that smoking caused heart disease, although some were more straightforward in their statements than others. The element of squirming under the spotlight that has distinguished tobacco companies in the past has been virtually eliminated. While they may never be covered in glory because of the nature of their product they have moved to make themselves at least acceptable.

Chris Ogden, of the Tobacco Manufacturers' Association, explains the against-all-odds success of the cigarette makers. 'Companies are well managed, tightly structured and highly mechanized with excellent industrial relations. Corporate social responsibility is high on their agenda and dealings with Government have been conducted openly through voluntary agreements and regular dialogue.

'The tobacco industry as a whole is exposed to close external scrutiny and conducts itself accordingly,' Ogden continues. 'The anti-smoking lobby is as vociferous as ever but, in a world where approximately one-third of adults choose to smoke, tobacco manufacturers will continue to survive and thrive as long as there is a demand for their products.'

Not every door was slammed in the face of the tobacco companies during the 1990s. Tobacco companies were boosted by the fall of

Communism and the consequent sale of many cigarette firms which were previously state-run monopolies. So Philip Morris now owns the whole of the Czech tobacco industry, once in the hands of its government.

Life has at times been extremely uncomfortable, though, for those involved in the tobacco industry. The outlook for tobacco companies was probably never more bleak than when the mechanism of the American state moved against them.

In 1996 the Attorney General of Washington filed a suit against tobacco companies for illegally targeting and marketing to minors, and also violating the state's consumer protection and anti-trust laws. And Washington was not alone. The tobacco companies found themselves facing the might of a vengeful American state system, with the prospect of an open-ended number of law suits pending.

The result was some earnest and detailed negotiation, which brought about the 1998 Master Settlement Agreement (MSA), signed by the attorneys general in 46 states and five US territories as well as by the movers and shakers of the tobacco industry. In brief, the MSA required participating tobacco companies to take down all billboard advertising on street corners and in sports arenas. It prohibited the use of cartoon characters to sell cigarettes and freed up state anti-tobacco campaigns and legislation from the prospect of legal action by the tobacco companies. For their part, the tobacco companies won protection from a volley of law suits – but the payoff line was a mighty $206 billion promised by the tobacco companies to the relevant states until the year 2025 to help rectify the harm caused by cigarettes. It's no surprise to learn that it is the largest settlement of its kind in legal history. Those tobacco companies that did not sign up to the agreement were nevertheless compelled by it to put money into a fund to help pay for future legal claims.

Large though the sum was, companies like British American Tobacco gave a guarded welcome to the MSA, believing the newly installed perimeters would restore stability to the listing industry. They saw it much like a tax. On the subject of litigation, tobacco companies view it as a manageable risk. The fact that cigarettes are harmful to health is widely known and, as such, that provides the grounds for a sturdy legal defence. Litigation has occurred

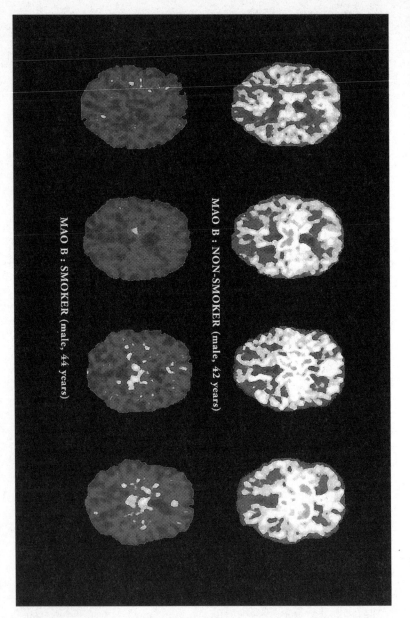

PET (Positron Emission Tomography) scans of the brains of a smoker (LEFT) and a non-smoker (RIGHT), showing the levels of monoamine oxidase B (MAO B), an enzyme that breaks down dopamine, a neurotransmitter chemical involved in motivation and behaviour. The smoker's brain is seen to have much lower levels of MAO B, which leads to higher levels of dopamine being present. As dopamine is involved in reinforcing behaviour, this may partly explain the addictive nature of tobacco smoking.

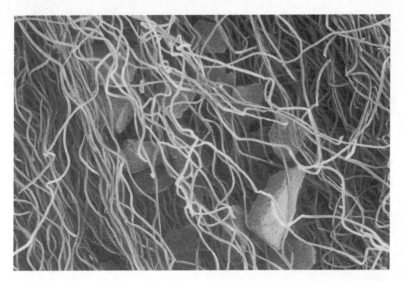

SEM (Scanning Electron Micrograph) shot of the filter of a cigarette. This filter contains acetate fibre and grains of charcoal, which help to remove toxic chemicals and unpleasant odours from the cigarette smoke.

Cigarettes are tested for the nicotine and tar content of their smoke for both medical research and as part of quality control in the tobacco industry. The cigarettes are being held vertically and having air sucked through them into the tubes in which their butts have been placed, where it will be analysed for its tar and nicotine content. Tar is one of the numerous toxic by-products released by the burning of cigarettes.

more frequently in the US than any other country because of the idiosyncracies of the legal system there, which are not replicated elsewhere. Philip Scourfield, assistant general counsel for litigation and regulation at BAT, pointed out, 'It is hot news that the tobacco industry has been targeted for consideration litigation activity. What frequently makes less news is that the vast majority of cases to date have been won by the industry.' In Brazil the tobacco company Souza Cruz has won all of the 74 cases brought against it.

But any optimism on the part of tobacco companies that the tide of litigation would be stemmed in the 21st century may have been premature. The World Health Organization intends to offer its expertise to those states and organizations that wish to take legal action against tobacco manufacturers. It is all part of a continuing campaign, outlined in a new report, *Towards Health With Justice*.

Furthermore, in Australia in April 2002 grandmother Rolah McCabe, 51, was awarded more than £260,000 ($380,000) by a court after it was found that a vast number of vital documents had been destroyed or hidden in a 'document retention' policy introduced by British American Tobacco in 1985. Anti-smokers believed the case would unleash a 'firestorm' of legal action in Australia. The issue of 'secret' documents held within the tobacco industry has regularly come back to haunt them.

As part of the MSA, the Commerce Committee of the House of Representatives in America forced tobacco companies to hand over 800 internal documents. The papers revealed that what these companies knew privately and what they said publicly were two different things. It was apparent that tobacco companies were aware of the risks attached to smoking for years but publicly denied that such hazards existed. According to the Committee, the documents unveiled 'a conspiracy of silence and suppression of scientific research'.

The damage done to the tobacco industry was extensive. Since then American researchers have discovered that the most effective campaigns to stop people smoking have been based on the presumed dishonesty of the tobacco companies.

Casting around for a redeemer, the tobacco industry bankrolled scientific programmes to bring about the advent of the 'safe' cigarette – a cigarette that leaves the smoker just as fulfilled as existing brands without the risk of catastrophic health effects. Despite years of investigation and investment, the unveiling of this universally popular safe cigarette still seems a distant event. It has proved devilishly difficult to rid cigarette smoke of its toxins while still maintaining an acceptable flavour. When tobacco substitutes were used the smoke was less toxic but the taste was undeniably synthetic. A range of different delivery systems has been tried. The production of a safe cigarette is by no means straightforward.

There are already brands and devices on the market which give the impression they reduce the health risks to smokers. RJ Reynolds has introduced Eclipse, Brown & Williamson has Advance, Philip Morris has produced Accord, while Omni is the product of Vector Tobacco. None has scaled the heights of popularity.

Traditionally tobacco companies have also been cagey about the development of safe cigarettes, for to concede that one was being engineered would be tacit admission that ordinary cigarettes were dangerous. Anti-smokers are also concerned about safe cigarettes, which could sidestep existing tobacco product legislation. Their argument is that any manner of delivery of nicotine and tar cannot be safe.

To reinforce this point, the American Legacy Foundation – funded by the MSA – played an April Fool's Day joke in 2002 by advertising on television the introduction of a 'safe' cigarette with the alluring name of Figment. The sales pitch went like this: 'Tobacco industry leaders met and agreed, together, that the time had come to create cigarettes free of poisons, carcinogens, and addictive nicotine,' a tobacco executive announced as he strolled through a laboratory. 'These are cigarettes that we can offer the public with confidence and with pride.'

The 'executive' and the new brand were, of course, hoaxes. 'For decades the tobacco industry misled the public into believing that low-tar or light cigarettes were safer for smokers,' explains Legacy President and Chief Executive Cheryl Healton. 'With this ad, we hoped to remind the public that there is no such thing as a safe cigarette.'

Whatever your view of them, it's worth knowing a little more about the world's leading tobacco companies. There are many firms dealing in tobacco products in the world so we'll just take a look at the biggest. These giant corporations have a habit of merging or fragmenting, changing their profile so often that it can be difficult to keep up on a regular basis so facts can move fast here.

The world's largest tobacco companies are, in descending order, Philip Morris, British American Tobacco, JT International, Imperial Tobacco, and Gallaher.

Philip Morris takes its name from the man who opened a tobacconist's shop in London's Bond Street in 1847. His grew to be a major family firm in Britain, which finally went public in 1881. Early in the 20th century the company expanded into America and has beavered its way out of relative obscurity to become an industry big hitter. Today it is the world leader in tobacco sales and its brands include Marlboro, Lark, and Parliament. Other companies in its stable include Miller Brewing, Nabisco, and Kraft foods. In 1999 Philip Morris revenues topped $78 billion (£47.5 billion) and its operating companies' income was $15.2 billion (£9.3 billion).

At present, British American Tobacco controls, among others, Rothmans, Lucky Strike, Kool, and Dunhill brands. It has enjoyed a colourful commercial history that began with the arrival in Britain at the start of the 20th century of Buck Duke, the head of the successful American Tobacco Company. With him he brought the technology for the mass production of cigarettes. But he was greeted with horror by buttoned-up

> Insurance companies have estimated that smoking a single cigarette lowers one's life expectancy by 10.7 minutes. That means in smoking a packet of 20 life is shortened by more than three and a half hours.

British businessmen when he announced, 'Hello boys, I'm Duke from New York, come to buy your business.'

In 1901, 13 British tobacco companies – including familiar names like Player's and Wills – merged to create Imperial with a view to fending off the rampant American corporations. But just a year later the hostilities of the trade war were forgotten in the interests of mutual gain and Imperial and American Tobacco joined together to create British American Tobacco, a dominant market force. Each agreed not to poach the other's domestic market and to support one another in overseas ventures. Chairing the new company was Buck Duke. Had it been allowed to continue the company might well have swallowed up all its opposition.

As it happened in 1911 the American Tobacco Company was judged to be a monopoly and Duke was compelled by the government to fragment the group. While Duke remained in the chair, British investors seized the opportunity to buy up newly available shares in British American Tobacco. As early as 1914, British American Tobacco also acquired the Brazilian company Souza Cruz, which remains a market leader even today.

An estimated 145 million people worldwide are directly or indirectly dependent on the tobacco industry for employment.

When Duke finally gave up the chair of BAT in 1923 the worldwide sales of cigarettes were greater than 25 billion sticks. The company went from strength to strength after buying the North Carolina company of Brown & Williamson. Three years later it swallowed up Rothmans, a business started in 1890 by Russian immigrant Louis Rothman who sold his own handmade cigarettes from a kiosk in London's Fleet Street. The support of influential press barons of the day ensured that Rothman thrived. He had even been granted a royal warrant and was busy with trade at home and overseas.

Decades later Imperial and Gallaher, another BAT buy-up, resumed their corporate identities and became independent once more. Imperial entered the tobacco superleague after acquiring the German tobacco company Reemtsma in 2002. The Imperial stable also includes Douwe Egberts van Nelle, Regals, Superkings, and Rizla cigarette papers.

In 1999 the royal warrant was withdrawn from Britain's big tobacco firm, Gallaher, probably because of the British royal family's no-smoking policy. Gallaher is the firm behind Berkley Superkings as well as Prestige Cookware and Whyte & Mackay whisky.

JT International was formed in 1999 when the Japan Tobacco Group bought RJ Reynolds. Its stable includes Winston, Camel, Mild Seven, and Salem. To discover more about JT International, you can now consult its web page on the Internet, where you can find its 'mission statement' which pledges 'to build a powerful global tobacco company, maximising value for our key stakeholders while striving for industry leadership. We will differentiate ourselves through sustained innovation in all areas and always deliver the best in consumer statistics.'

When questioned most closely about the company's views on young smokers, their response was short: 'Unfortunately, we really have only one message for teenagers and that is: "Don't smoke". We try not to be involved in any media that is addressed primarily at those under 18.'

By contrast, its competitors among the big tobacco companies embraced the discussion around the dilemma of young smokers full-on. JT International's attitude might have been typical of big tobacco corporations a decade ago but no longer. No one finds corporate blind obstinacy an asset these days.

Most of the major companies have a stake in the familiar brand of Benson & Hedges. Gallaher owns the brand in Britain which has been the nation's most popular cigarette, BAT has possession of it in most of the Pacific, the Middle East, Africa, and the European duty-free market, while Philip Morris own the rights in the US and Canada. Silk Cut is also subject to this kind of identity split.

The total production of tobacco worldwide in 2001 amounted to 5.7 million tonnes grown in more than 120 countries. The top five producers, in descending order, are China, the United States, India, Brazil, and Turkey.

Hard to believe that so much has evolved out of so little, for the humble tobacco plant, Nicotiana, is not remarkable in appearance and grows freely. Part of the nightshade plant family, it is a cousin of the potato and the pepper. Growing naturally in North and South America, Australia and the Pacific, it has been imported into Europe, Asia, and Africa. There are different types of tobacco plant and the one indigenous to Australia differs from that in America. It is common tobacco, *Nicotiana tabacum*, that was taken by Rolfe from the West Indies to Virginia to launch the tobacco industry, while wild tobacco, *Nicotiana rustica*, was favoured by Native Americans.

If left untended, plants grow to between four and six feet in height (one to two metres) and bear flowers of pink or white. It is the leaves, though, that are of interest to the smoker and these vary in potency, flavour, and smoking suitability between species and even on an individual plant. Lower leaves, for example, tend to yield less in the way of nicotine.

Before they can be used the midrib of the leaf is stripped out. Tobacco is then cured by air, fire, or flue. Air-cured tobacco is stored in mechanically ventilated buildings for one or two months. With fire curing the tobacco is suspended above open wood fires which burn intermittently for between three and ten weeks. Flue curing takes place in small barns heated by metal pipes extending from furnaces around or under the floor. It takes just four to eight days.

When the leaves are dry but not crumbly they are graded, packed up in bales or packages and delivered to auction warehouses, where they are bought by leaf buyers or manufacturers. A cigarette maker looks for variety and is likely to pursue a further drying process. Indeed, most tobacco products are blended so that manufacturers can achieve uniformity in taste and texture.

As it happens, tobacco thrives in regions with poor soils and difficult weather patterns, making it ideal for land in the developing nations. It is often the farmer's choice because other crops would fare badly in the same spot. Planting, tending and harvesting of tobacco remains a labour-intensive industry. The tobacco industry attracts criticism from environmentalists concerned at the fertilizer, herbicides,

More than 105 billion cigarettes are sold every week – that's ten million per minute.

and pesticides lavished on the crop. In addition the curing process eats up immense amounts of coal, oil, or timber. One critical estimate has it that for every acre of tobacco produced an acre of woodland is exhausted.

Producers across the world have a voice in the International Tobacco Growers' Association (ITGA), formed in 1984 and now representative of farmers from 22 countries producing 85 per cent of the world's traded leaf tobacco. It speaks for more than 35 million people involved in the growing and early stage processing of the crop in countries as diverse as Cyprus, India, Kenya and Venezuela. Most are small-scale farmers who may not have the appropriate weapons in their armoury to fend off large organizations like the World Health Organization (WHO), pursuing a tobacco-control policy. From the ITGA comes guidance and advice for growers on a wide range of issues. It only talks tobacco on agricultural grounds and avoids the pro-/anti-smoking debate.

Action by the WHO has angered those in the ITGA. 'Our industry faces its greatest ever global challenge with WHO, supported by the World Bank, leading the 'anti' campaign to suffocate markets and drive us all out of business,' said Zimbabwean Richard Tate when he was president. 'Fighting this common cause has brought all the stakeholders in our industry together in support of the tobacco grower.' However, the ITGA emphatically denies links with cigarette manufacturers or being an 'industry-front organization' and insists it has the condition of tobacco growers at the top of its agenda.

The main importers of tobacco leaf are the United States, Germany, the Russian Federation, the United Kingdom, Holland, and Japan.

In Malawi, where 140,000 tonnes was produced, the price per kilo in 2001 was $1.09 (£073), disappointingly low for farmers. Nevertheless, tobacco cultivation and sale still represents an overall income of some $165 million (£110.5 billion) to this poverty-stricken country and employs some 532,000 people.

Like other Third World countries, Malawi defends its right to grow the crop despite the sensitivities of the Western world. Paul Kwengwere, a communications officer with Action Aid, explained that to date the developed world's approach has been somewhat simplistic. 'Contrary to expectations from tobacco lobbyists, Malawi maintains its protection of the industry because up to now tobacco has been the back of Malawi's economy. The industry commands about 70 per cent of export earnings and it is estimated that over 50 per cent of the Malawian population derive their livelihood from the tobacco industry.

'To an extent the government has a point in protecting the industry because, while people have preached against tobacco, very little has been done in coming up with alternative crops that can easily substitute tobacco in terms of financial benefits.

'Unlike quite a few countries tobacco smoking is not very high in Malawi. Out of the tobacco produced – which is usually in the range of about 150kg million per annum – only two per cent is consumed in Malawi. This is only about 3kg million (6.6lb million), a figure so small that BAT stopped manufacturing cigarettes in Malawi in 1998 because they found it more expensive to maintain their machines than to import and pack.'

Industry observers keep a keen eye on the effect of instability in Zimbabwe, where some 200,000 tonnes have traditionally been produced each year. Many of the Zimbabwean farmers terrorized by war veterans are tobacco growers.

The production of tobacco to feed the world's nicotine addiction may involve child labour in the developing world. As many as 250 million children under the age of 14 across the globe are believed to be shackled to low- paid jobs. A good proportion will be at work in the tobacco fields when they should be at their schoolbooks or at play. This is particularly true in Africa where the AIDS epidemic has stripped families of adult workers. It is also known that bidis, the hand-rolled, flavoured cigarettes from India that have found favour with American adolescents' are produced by child labour. Attorney generals in the USA have voiced their concern about the status of labourers involved in bidi production as well as the health risks the cigarette poses.

In response, the Elimination of Child Labor in Tobacco Growing Foundation was launched in October 2000. Behind it lies the might of British American Tobacco, the International Tobacco Growers' Association and the International Union of Food, Agricultural, Hotel, Restaurant, Catering, Tobacco, and Allied Workers' Associations.

This well-intentioned initiative from the West has been received with caution. As Kwengwere in Malawi explained, 'There has been some research in education sectors where it has been found that primary school's low attendance (in tobacco growing districts) during certain periods of the year is linked to tobacco harvest or processing.

'However, despite the available findings, Tobacco Association of Malawai (TAMA) has insisted that children only help in tobacco processing during holiday and after school hours and it does not think child labour is an issue. In fact they have been defending such activities by equating them to petty jobs in developed countries where children are employed as babysitters, in delivering newspapers and milk, in restaurants, shops, family businesses, or washing cars.'

But the problems of smoking in the Western world may soon be visited on underdeveloped nations, according to tobacco analysts.

'They got lips, we want them.' These six little words that fell from the mouth of a tobacco-company executive are held up banner-style by anti-smoking groups as a prime example of corporate callousness. This oft-quoted executive was talking some years ago in terms of the youth market. His comment is applicable today to the Third World, where the numbers of people now smoking is about to explode.

Some cultures in Asia and Africa have traditionally frowned upon women smoking. That is all about to change, as globalization brings Western virtues and vices into their backyards. Tobacco companies are sponsoring disco nights and sports events at which cigarettes are freely distributed. Typically those employed to do the distributing are gorgeous girls clad in sought-after fashions, making cigarettes seem as sophisticated as they are in the West.

These smokers-in-waiting are poor – but the cigarettes sold in the Third World in fives or even singly don't cost a great deal. In many of these countries health education is at a minimum. Given waves of crises that hit the Third World, including famine, the deadly Ebola virus and the AIDS epidemic, the illnesses brought about by smoking seem the least of their problems.

'About 40 per cent of America's 50 million smokers will try to give up the habit at least once this year.' Center for Disease Control and Prevention.

It is not only in the Third World that farmers defend their rights to make money from a long-standing cash crop. Another front in the US battle against nicotine is the introduction of cash subsidies designed to phase out tobacco farming. It has long been an important crop in America with 21 states growing it, the biggest crops coming in from Kentucky and North Carolina. The 'don't grow' incentive came as part of the 1998 Master Settlement Agreement in which the tobacco industry agreed to contribute cash for health, education and other programmes. Some of this money was earmarked to help shrink the highly profitable business of tobacco cultivation. (However, the European Union continues to subsidize Europe's tobacco farmers with millions of pounds each year to produce the crop.)

In Maryland, at least two-thirds of the state's 991 tobacco farmers signed up for the handout and more were expected to follow suit in subsequent years. But these have thrown up some unexpected side effects that are undermining the initiative, namely among Amish farmers in Maryland.

The Amish are conservative Christians descended from European immigrants who eschew modern conveniences. They drive a horse and buggy in place of a car, they wear long, black, homemade clothing fastened with hooks and eyes rather than buttons or zippers and they choose to ignore modern developments like the telephone and electricity. Nor would they accept government grants to change the methods of farming they have pursued over generations. Now non-Amish competitors in the tobacco-growing regions are falling away, leaving the Amish farmers to reap peak prices for their harvest. And they are considering planting more tobacco than ever before.

> 'Smoking is a matter of informed adult choice. Whilst there are many controversial issues surrounding tobacco, it is still legal to manufacture, buy, sell, and use tobacco products.' Chris Ogden, Tobacco Manufacturers' Association.

There's long been concern that the restriction or annihilation of the tobacco industry would result in significant job losses both in manufacturing and retail across the planet and thus make a detrimental impact on numerous national economies.

The counter-argument is that domestic economies, mainly in the West, are dented by smokers. The cost of smoking extends to working days lost to sickness and a dip in productivity caused by smoking breaks. More than 430,000 people die in America each year from smoking-related causes and the annual cost of these preventable illnesses in healthcare expenditures and lost productivity is more than $97 billion (£65 billion).

It is difficult to assess whether smokers are a national burden in terms of health costs because their life span tends to be shorter. The cost to their countries are telescoped into a shorter length of time.

While smoking causes diseases and lost work days in the West, these countries continue to import the raw materials. The main importers of tobacco leaf are the United States, Germany, the Russian Federation, the

United Kingdom, Holland, and Japan. These are not only major cigarette manufacturers and consumers but export the finished product as well.

Not only do richer countries pay with their health, some pay with their pocket too. While the price of cigarettes varies worldwide and from region to region, a packet comes cheaper in places where tobacco is grown and is expensive in countries where governments have made a concerted effort to tax it out of fashion.

The cheapest place in Europe to have a smoke is Turkey. Go to Italy and the same cigarettes so cheaply available in Turkey will cost about four times as much while smokers in Norway will pay double the amount charged to the Italians. Norway, where the twin evil of alcohol is also notoriously pricey, is probably the most expensive country in the world in which to smoke, although England ranks highly, too.

Worldwide, cigarettes are cheap in Indonesia, Malaysia, Taiwan, and Panama. In Switzerland the price is similar to that in Texas which is more expensive than Japan but cheaper than Israel.

The high level of tax in Britain masks the true cost of cigarettes. Consumers don't query the amount they have to pay because it is hidden by the rate of tax, which accounts for between 80 and 90 per cent of the pack price. It is far higher than other goods that are likewise seen as luxury items. In 2002 the duty on beer stood at 29 per cent, on wine at 51 per cent, spirits at 61 per cent, and unleaded petrol at 75 per cent. The money reaped from cigarette taxation amounts to almost half of the British defence budget. The culture of soaraway cigarette prices covers up the fact that they are still a highly profitable commodity. High profit margins also help reduce the threat of a brand war.

Tobacco is not grown commercially in Britain so all the tobacco leaf used in manufactured cigarettes must be imported. But once the leaf has been turned into cigarettes and associated products there's enough to supply the home market and plenty left over for export. This market alone is worth some £900 million ($1.3 billion) to Britain. Subtract the cost of importing the tobacco leaf and the balance remains at about £586 million ($856 million) in Britain's favour.

However, cigarette sales in Britain have tumbled of late. Between 1993 and 2000 sales were down by about 38 per cent. The fall reflects not only the fact that Britons are smoking less and that smuggling has substantially increased, depressing official sales figures, but also that more people than ever before are rolling their own to sidestep cigarette costs.

Nevertheless the total tobacco consumption in the United Kingdom remains staggeringly high. In 2000 the Brits puffed their way through 56 billion cigarettes, 2.8kg million of hand-rolling and pipe tobacco, and 900 million cigars. For the record there are 300 cigarette brands on sale in Britain, although the top ten commandeered some 60 per cent of the market.

In 2000 Europe produced 742,143 million cigarettes, 7,053 million cigars, 21,730 million tonnes of pipe tobacco, and 74,594 million tonnes of rolling tobacco. The number of jobs related to the tobacco industry in Europe amounted to 1,379,779.

In Europe some 605,483 million cigarettes were consumed by 93.45 million smokers during 2000.

One major source of irritation to non-smoking groups in Britain is that tax revenue amounted to £7.5 billion ($11 billion) when anti-smoking programmes were being financed to the tune of £40 million ($58.4 million). More money should be diverted to helping smokers quit, they argue.

Precisely the same issue upsets clean-living folk across the Atlantic where cigarettes come in at around half the price of those in Britain. For years the anti-smoking lobby believed that, if the government was serious about tackling the problem of teenage smoking, it would raise the price of a packet so it was beyond the reach of the average youngster. American studies show that for every ten per cent increase in the price of cigarettes there will be a reduction of seven per cent in the numbers of young people smoking and an overall drop in cigarette consumption of between three to five per cent. Only in the later years of the Clinton administration were their wishes granted.

Smuggling cigarettes into Britain is a lucrative business and one that is costing the Treasury dearly. According to the HM Customs, one in five of the 78 billion cigarettes smoked a year in Britain – 15.6 billion to those of you who don't have calculator brains – are smuggled into the country avoiding the payment of duty. The loss to the country is something in the order of £3.5 billion ($5.1 billion) each year.

Smuggling has also put a squeeze on corner shops that have depended on smokers popping in for a packet of cigarettes and perhaps picking up a newspaper, pint of milk and a chocolate bar at the same time. When smokers discover an alternative source for cigarettes – the man down the pub, for example, or the market trader – they don't go into the corner shop at all.

In Britain, the Tobacco Alliance represents more than 21,000 independent retailers across the UK. It is funded by the Tobacco Manufacturers' Association. The Alliance opposes the burden of tax placed on British smokers who pay a greater penalty on cigarettes and hand-rolling tobacco than any other country in Europe. To support its argument it quotes the eminent economist and philosopher Adam Smith (1723–90) who wrote in his *Wealth Of Nations*, 'An injudicious tax offers a great temptation to smuggling.'

Furthermore, it claims, a popular brand of cigarettes that sold for £4.39 ($6.41) in the UK was available for just £1.90 ($2.76) in Belgium. (Of the packet price, some £3.46 [$5.06] goes straight to the government in tax.) Hand-rolling tobacco costs four times as much in Britain as it does in Belgium. With this kind of financial incentive bootleggers are enticed to continue running tobacco supplies. Indeed, some authorities are concerned that cigarette smugglers can afford to lose substantial consignments to the customs men and still remain profitable. And every time taxes are hiked the smugglers work harder and reap greater benefits. By way of example, look at the IRA, whose activities include, among others, smuggling tobacco into Britain and Eire. Analysts believe the organization reaps up to £7 million ($10.2 million) per year mostly from contraband cigarettes brought in from Eastern Europe by the lorry load but also from fake brand-name whiskies from the Far East. According to *The Sunday Times* on 28 April 2002, 'By avoiding customs duties the IRA can sell the smuggled cigarettes at attractive prices on the black market and still make up to £400,000 ($584,400) profit on each load.

Light and easy to transport, cigarettes are a much more portable contraband than other products, such as alcohol.

British MP Kevin Barron told the House of Commons in June 2000, 'We are told that the scale of the profits that can be made from cigarette smuggling is comparable with the profits made from drug smuggling, and that criminals are turning to cigarette smuggling because the risks and penalties are lower than those that apply with drugs.'

At a later date, Barron told the House, 'There is no doubt that it is much easier for young children to get their hands on smuggled tobacco than it is for them to buy tobacco from retail outlets.'

One MP used strong words to shatter the illusion that tobacco smuggling was a crime in which no one got hurt. As Financial Secretary to the Treasury, Paul Boateng said, 'Smuggling on this scale is not a victimless crime that does no one any harm but it is highly organized criminal gangs that are involved. It attacks the livelihood of legitimate traders and in particular makes cigarettes and alcohol cheaper and more accessible to children.'

Given that Britain has neither the manpower nor the resources to eradicate smuggling, there's vocal support for a lowering of duty on cigarettes to bring prices in line with the rest of Europe. In doing so, the government would grievously undermine the black market. In Canada, where for this reason the price of cigarettes was reduced, the government benefited from increased revenue as hordes of people stopped smuggling cigarettes from the United States.

In America the smuggling of cigarettes is dealt with by the Bureau of Alcohol, Tobacco, and Firearms. Anyone carrying 60,000 cigarettes or more without evidence of having paid state taxes is presumed to be a smuggler.

In the States the problem is often internal, a case of smuggling cigarettes from North Carolina, for example, where they are taxed at 50¢ (33p) a carton, to resell in Michigan, where the tax stands at $7.50 (£5) a carton. There have been allegations that terrorist groups from the Middle East have been financing operations in this way.

Whatever the cost of cigarettes, think of the money you'd save if you quit. Let's take as an example a British smoker on 20 a day. Of course, the figures vary by brand and outlet but the savings could add up to about £130 ($190) per month or £1,600 ($2,338) per year. That's the cost of a foreign holiday, a takeaway meal once a week for a year or a wardrobe

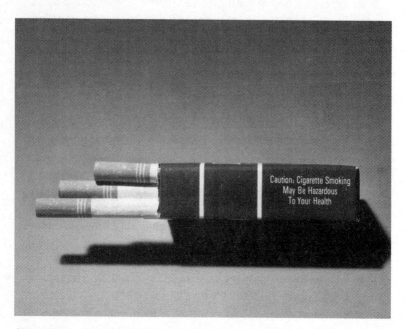

Since 1 January 1966, packs of cigarettes have been required to feature a health warning, which typically reads, 'Caution: Cigarette Smoking May Be Hazardous To Your Health'.

Two young boys smoking. The young are seen by the tobacco industry as a new market, the lifeblood of cigarette sales, a demographic required to offset the fall-off in sales incurred by the deaths of older customers.

of new clothes. The financially astute ex-smoker will invest this tidy sum to make it work harder. One financial newspaper claimed that a smoker who gave up a decade ago would be picking up a cheque in the order of £20,000 ($29,220).

Then there is the money that the nation would save. The Royal College of Physicians used the value of a human life deduced by the Department of Transport to work out the financial cost of smoking. One life was said to be worth £680,590.20 ($994,342), bringing the cost of smoking-related mortality in the UK at 1997 figures to just under £80 billion ($117 billion).

The comparative figures are much lower for the American smoker because cigarettes cost less. But in the US reformed smokers might reap financial benefits in other ways.

In America, insurance benefits fall into the lap of people who have never smoked and, to a lesser extent, those who have quit. Insurers differentiate between those who have never touched a cigarette, people who gave up smoking a long time ago, recent quitters, light smokers and heavy smokers.

There are many hidden cash rewards for non-smokers and the main one comes from health insurance. Just about all the policies available are cheaper for those people who don't smoke. In some cases life insurance cover for smokers is twice the amount of an identical deal for non-smokers.

There's some good news, too, for smokers from the insurance world, albeit tinged with doom. Insurers will sometimes give preferential terms to smokers when they convert pension funds into lifetime annuities, which yield regular income. The reason is simple. Insurance companies know that the average smoker will die sooner than the average non-smoker so they can afford to be that bit more generous in rates.

The same goes for household insurance – but for different reasons. House fires are a major cause of losses in this field and one of the primary sources of domestic blazes is the humble butt. (The cost of house fires, both material and human, runs into millions of pounds each year.)

Indeed, many countries have paid dearly for fires caused by matches or cigarettes. On 18 November 1987 a fireball ripped through King's Cross Underground station in London, killing 31 people and leaving many others with physical and mental scars that will never heal. The cause was believed to be a match or cigarette butt, which ignited gases lurking in the nether reaches of the underground escalators.

This is just one, albeit spectacular, example of how cigarettes and associated materials can ruin lives. Major national catastrophes, ecological disasters like the bush fires of Australia and countless thousands of domestic tragedies across the world have been caused by an ill-placed dog-end.

Stacie Demaraise, from the US National Fire Protection Association, revealed some startling figures which put the blame for most house blazes squarely on the shoulders of cigarette smokers: 'During 1994–98 73 per cent of residential smoking-material fires and 64 per cent of associated civilian deaths were caused by careless disposal of smoking materials. When you add this to other misuses of smoking materials (falling asleep with a lit cigarette, cigar or pipe, drug or alcohol impairment) the figures become 86 per cent for fires and 91 per cent for deaths.' To compare, only two per cent of residential fire deaths were as a result of suspicious circumstances – for example, arson.

> Martin Broughton, the executive chairman of British American Tobacco, was catapulted into the news in 2002 after admitting he advised his two children not to smoke because of the health risks. Speaking after the announcement of pre-tax annual profits of £2 billion ($2.922 billion) he revealed that he had said to his children, '[Smoking] is not good for you.' Furthermore, he restricts himself to an occasional cigar.

The NFPA wants to see increased public fire safety education hand in glove with successful smoking cessation programmes. Smokers who enjoy a puff in bed without using sturdy, large ashtrays are the fireman's pet hate. 'It is essential to have programmes that will focus on careless behaviour because it is such a large part of the smoking-material fire problem.'

It wants to see cigarettes carrying a fire warning alongside the health notice. One state, New York, has already taken steps to see that this happens. In addition, it favours the redesign of cigarettes to reduce their propensity to ignite other items. Entire new business strategies have already been built around the risks posed by sparks from cigarette ends, as Demaraise explains: 'In the '70s and early '80s, efforts to reduce smoking-material fires were focused on modifying the items most frequently ignited by smoking materials – mattresses and upholstered furniture. These new products were designed using materials more resistant to cigarette ignitions. Since those initiatives there have been major reductions in the number of fires involving upholstered furniture and mattresses.' But, she warned, 'This initiative alone is not enough to ensure a continued decrease in smoking-material fires and fire deaths. And although these products are more resistant to ignitions by smoking materials, some may burn faster or more intensely or produce more toxic smoke once ignited.'

While fire deaths from burning cigarette butts are declining, there's still more to be done: 'In the past few years, it has seemed that an out-and-out war has been declared on cigarette smoking,' said Demaraise. 'Whole towns have banned smoking in public buildings and some have even made it a crime for minors to possess cigarettes. There is a major radio and television public education campaign going on to try to reduce cigarette smoking across the US. These actions will ultimately have a positive impact on future smoking-material fires. But is it enough?

'Public education is also needed to address the risks of smoking and fires. Everyone should be made aware of the danger of smoking-material fires and not just the smokers themselves.'

Russia, too, has overhauled its laws regarding cigarettes in the 21st century. Now almost all forms of tobacco advertising are banned and smoking is not permitted in many public places outside designated areas. All flights lasting under three hours are non-smoking.

For the first time, tar and nicotine levels in Russian cigarettes are to be published. The maximum tar in a filter cigarette is 14mg while in a non-filter the figure is 16mg. Filter cigarettes can no longer exceed 1.2mg of nicotine or 1.3mg in non-filters. Vending machines have been outlawed along with packs of ten cigarettes and selling to anyone under the age of 18. Smoking must be an essential part of the plot if a cigarette is to appear in TV programmes, in theatres, or on the big screen.

As for the future, are the tobacco companies in real jeopardy from the world becoming a smoke-free zone? '[It's] unlikely for as long as people are free to make their own lifestyle choices,' said Chris Ogden, from the TMA. 'Bans don't work *viz* prohibition in the USA. For the future, the tobacco industry is likely to see both consolidation in terms of mergers and acquisitions and expansion in terms of increasing globalization of company operations.'

ADDITIONAL INFO

'If I cannot smoke cigars in Heaven then I shall not go.' - Mark Twain

'The average consumption of cigarettes by male and female smokers in Britain is currently 16 and 14 cigarettes per day respectively, a figure which has changed little over the past 20 years.' - Royal College of Physicians

Imagine a society without cigarettes. Would we all be sweet-smelling, sporty types living long, productive lives? The answer has to be maybe, yes. At least we must acknowledge that we stand a better chance of doing that if we don't smoke.

But cigarettes and smokers are not going to go away. Business empires are built around them, social orders are rooted in them. Smoking has a four hundred year history in the West that cannot be obliterated. Upon these solid, centuries-old foundations the habit of smoking has thrown up glorious edifices and no amount of anti-smoking propaganda appears to be able to bring the house down.

Smoking is one of the most troubling aspects of modern life. There are numerous threads leading into tightly bound arguments from both sides. You can deeply offend people by smoking but others get the hump if you are a devout anti-smoker. Your opinion counts, and sometimes it counts against you.

Smoking caused a spat at an old people's home in Stretford, Manchester, where walking sticks were brandished in anger and the police were called. The events at the sheltered housing complex were a fascinating parochial insight into an international issue.

Thirty-seven residents out of a total of 46 didn't smoke. A woman seeking a clean air ruling in the communal lounge – a former smoker – said cigarette smoke aggravated her asthma and bronchitis. Fair enough.

Yet those nine smokers organized a ballot, which they won by 19 votes to eight with 11 abstentions. Somehow the matter switched from being about smoking to those dearly held values of freedom. This time liberty was an outright winner. Having interviewed everyone involved the police decided to take no further action. But this image of false teeth clattering in anger, of wrinkled fists flying, of purple perms going awry illustrates the problem with smoking. People, old and young, get mad about it.

Secretary Maeve Sullivan, from south London, believes herself a typical example of a woman smoker. 'I started smoking because I thought it was cool. It was a way of being perceived as a young woman rather than a child. I became a heavy smoker, getting through at least 20 and sometimes 40 cigarettes a day. I gave up once when I had a relationship with someone who was vehemently anti-smoking, then I got drunk, had a cigarette and the next day I was back on 20 a day. I stopped a second time when I got pregnant. Both times I exercised to make sure I didn't put on weight. For me it was a lifestyle change.

'I have no intention of starting again. It puts years on your complexion. As they say, if your lungs were on the outside you wouldn't smoke. Now I'm really against smoking.'

She favours an all-out war on smoking. 'People who smoke are in denial. They don't want to be confronted with stark, hideous reality. I made myself read some really harsh statistics about cancer and that helped.

'I'm against prohibition but I would like to see cigarette prices rise again. I support the banning of tobacco advertising, too. All too often attractive people are portrayed smoking. It is still considered to be glamorous among young women as well as a form of rebellion. Now people can get help to stop smoking on prescription. That has got to be the way forward.'

But she is concerned about the vocal condemnation of people who fall ill after smoking. 'People can be very judgemental. For many, smoking is their only pleasure. We should be making our feelings known to the government, not the individual.'

On the other side of the fence stands British American Tobacco, the epitome of corporate rationality.

'At British American Tobacco, we have long accepted that smoking is risky. Our business is not about persuading people to smoke; it is about offering quality brands to adults who have already taken the decision to smoke. We strongly believe that smoking should only be for adults who are aware of the risks.

'British American Tobacco companies produce fine quality products that provide pleasure to many millions of adult smokers around the world. Along with the pleasures of cigarette smoking come real risks of serious diseases such as lung cancer, respiratory disease and heart disease. We also recognize that, for many people, it is difficult to quit smoking.

'Put simply, smoking is a cause of certain diseases. This has been the working hypothesis of much of our product modification research, has been believed by smokers for decades and is the most appropriate viewpoint for consumers and public health authorities.

'The risks associated with smoking are primarily defined by epidemiological studies that show that groups of lifetime smokers have far higher incidence of certain diseases than comparable groups of non-smokers. These risks tend to be greater in groups that start smoking younger, smoke for longer, smoke more cigarettes per day and, to some extent, smoke high-tar cigarettes compared to those who consume less tar. The statistics, however, do not tell us whether a particular individual smoker will avoid an associated disease by smoking less or smoking lower-tar cigarettes. Moreover, all smoking behaviours are associated with some risk, and the only way to be sure to avoid a smoking-related risk is not to smoke.'

Tobacco is a bogey of health education, but it isn't alone. One American woman lamented on national television that it took her just three years to quit smoking. It has taken her far longer to conquer her other craving, for sugar and sweet things. Reports about the dangers of sugar overload on today's society vibrate with spooky echoes of those early warnings issued about cigarettes. The jury is still out on how dangerous excess sugar can be.

Every attempt has been made to drive smoking out of the public eye yet there has been no corresponding plunge in the number of smokers.

For Sir Richard Doll, who devoted most of his life to proving the hazards posed by smoking, it is disappointing and baffling that society continues to smoke: 'A lot of people have given up. We have seen the mortality from lung cancer come down. But it is discouraging that the government has taken a number of steps, but to no avail. The prospect for the future is not as bright as one would have hoped.

'Young people of both sexes are taking it up as frequently as they did in the past. Sometimes it is a matter of a dare, or they are doing what their parents do. And if a 20-year-old is doing something, a 15-year-old will want to do it too.'

It's not even as if all smokers are happy. When it comes to quitting smoking, writer Mark Asher is a veteran. Despite numerous attempts he has been unable to kick the habit and it leaves him with an overwhelming sense of irony: 'You've got to hand it to tobacco companies. What other industry or business can kill its customers and not worry about it because there are plenty more punters on the horizon? (I grant you that some fast-food outlets probably do the same thing.)

'What is it about smoking? Where is the appeal in a product that is clearly labelled "I will harm you" or even "I will kill you"? And where exactly do governments sit on this one when you tally up the immense tax generated through the Treasury by a year-on-year rise in tax on the old cancer sticks. Those of us that smoke are perversely helping to fund the NHS and will equally cripple it with smoking-related diseases.

'The plain fact of the matter is that smoking is not pleasurable, only addictive. It is a socially acceptable drug that has you reaching for your pocket and leaves you out of pocket.'

Health education is a wonderful thing. No one lives in houses with asbestos roofs these days. The peril of dirty drinking water has been eradicated. Lead is no longer used in paint.

Research has shown us the way forward on numerous subjects but its success has always been dependent on common cooperation. If the majority of the general public accepts the colossal body of investigative papers that claims smoking is deadly then cigarettes and associated products will one day be consigned to history and viewed as quaint vices, rather like eating with your fingers or pouring buckets of urine out of top-floor windows into the street below. Once nobody gave these bizarre practices a second thought. While smoking is construed as a matter of civil liberty and personal pleasure it is sure to remain with us for some years to come.

GLOSSARY

Alcopops – Soft drinks flavoured with alcohol

Annuities – Investment funds issuing annual returns

ATF – Bureau of Alcohol, Tobacco and Firearms, responsible for stopping cigarette smuggling in the US

DNA – Short for deoxyribonucleic acid. DNA is found in chromosomes and carries genetic information which helps the body to work

Dopamine – Neurotransmitter that creates pleasure pathways in the brain, the production of which is prompted by nicotine

Epidemiology – Statistically led science that investigates the incidence and causes of diseases that are associated with a particular environment or way of life

IRA – Irish Republican Army, a terrorist group operating in Northern Ireland

ITGA – International Tobacco Growers' Association, formed in 1984 to represent tobacco farmers

NFPA – National Fire Protection Association, an American organization devoted to cutting the number of blazes

saltpetre – potassium nitrate, a white crystalline substance added to cigarette paper to make it burn

TAMA – Tobacco Association of Malawi

WHO – World Health Organization, an active anti-smoking body

TIMELINE

1492: Columbus discovers New World and tobacco

1531: European cultivation of tobacco begins in Santo Domingo

1548: Commercial cultivation of tobacco begins in Brazil

1556: Jean Nicot de Villemain sends tobacco to France and gives his name to nicotine

1590: Papal bull issued, excommunicating anyone who uses snuff in church

1600: Sir Walter Raleigh persuades Queen Elizabeth I to sample smoking

1604: King James I issues *A Counterblaste To Tobacco*

1612: First tobacco plantation established in the US

1617: Pocahontas, the Indian princess who helped European settlers to find a treatment for tobacco, dies on the way to England

1619: First African workers arrive in Jamestown

1620: Some 40,000lb (18,144kg) of tobacco imported from Virginia to England

1624: New York founded as New Amsterdam on a site known to Native Americans as 'tobacco fields'

1660: Charles II restored to British throne and introduces practice of snuff-taking

1661: Slavery legalized in Virginia

1665: Smoking becomes compulsory for boys at Eton School, England

1675: Tobacco Chamber instituted in Berne, Switzerland, to punish suspected smokers

1724: Pope Benedict XIII learns to smoke and overturns papal opposition to tobacco

1746: Nicotine and water first used as an insecticide

1750: About 145,000 slaves are working on the tobacco plantations in America

1760: Pierre Lorillard establishes a 'manufactory' to mass-produce pipe tobacco, cigars and snuff

1761: Dr John Hill warns that snuff takers risk cancer of the nose

1776: Tobacco helps to finance American Revolution

1826: England imports 250,000lb (113,398kg) of cigars a year

1828: Nicotine isolated for the first time from the tobacco plant

1832: Egyptian soldiers credited with making the modern cigarette

1847: Philip Morris opens a shop in England selling hand-rolled Turkish cigars and tobacco

1852: Matches are produced

1853-6: Crimean War. British soldiers imitate Turkish allies in cigarette smoking

1854: Philip Morris makes his first cigarette

1856: The health implications of smoking are discussed in the British medical journal *The Lancet*

1864: First American cigarette factory opens

1873: Philip Morris dies. His company is taken over by widow Margaret and brother Leopold

1875: RJ Reynolds opens a chewing-tobacco company

1875: Picture cards are first used to stiffen flimsy packets of cigarettes

1876: Benson & Hedges receives a royal warrant

1880: Bonsack cigarette machine is patented

1884: Using the Bonsack machine, Duke Buchanan produces an annual total of 744 million cigarettes

1889: James Buchanan (Buck) Duke merges five companies to form American Tobacco Company

1889: Lung cancer cases worldwide amount to an estimated 140

1890: Louis Rothman begins selling cigarettes in London's Fleet Street

1894: Brown & Williamson form a partnership in Winston-Salem producing plug, snuff, and pipe tobacco

1900: Pall Mall launched

1901: Philip Morris granted a royal warrant as tobacconist to King Edward VII

1902: Philip Morris moves to the US. British American Tobacco Company formed

1904: Cigarette coupons are introduced

1913: Formation of American Society for the Control of Cancer, forerunner of the American Cancer Society. RJ Reynolds launches Camel cigarettes

1927: British American Tobacco takes control of Brown & Williamson

1932: Zippo lighter invented by George G Blaisdell

1933: Brown & Williamson introduce the menthol cigarette Kool in opposition to existing menthol cigarette on market, Spud

1939: German scientists make a link between smoke inhalation and lung cancer

1940: Top-selling brands in America in descending order are Camel, Lucky Strike, Chesterfield, Raleigh, Old Gold, and Pall Mall

1950: *Journal Of The American Medical Association* publishes Ernst Wynder's work on smoking and lung cancer

1951: Popular TV series *I Love Lucy* launched, sponsored by Philip Morris

1953: Wynder establishes biological link between smoking and cancer

1954: Marlboro cowboy created by Chicago advertising agency Leo Burnett for Philip Morris

1955: RJ Reynolds launches Salem, the first filter-tipped menthol cigarette

1956: Philip Morris introduce the flip-top box

1957: US Surgeon General Leroy E Burney becomes first federal official to talk about smoking and cancer

1958: Actor Humphrey Bogart dies of lung cancer

1962: US places embargo on Cuba, making import of Cuban cigars illegal. Royal College of Physicians publish report *Smoking And Health*

1967: US Federal Trade Commission releases first tar and nicotine report

1967: Action on Smoking and Health founded

1968: Virginia Slims launched by Philip Morris

1968: First Formula One racing teams accept tobacco sponsorship

1969: Cigarette Act of 1969 bans tobacco advertising from radio and TV in the US

1969: Philip Morris acquires the Miller Brewing Company

1970: Finnair provides non-smoking seats on its flights

1971: Joseph Cullman, from Philip Morris, appears on TV programme *Face The Nation* to be confronted with findings from a study which said smoking mothers gave birth to smaller babies. 'Some women would prefer having smaller babies,' he replies

1972: Health warning 'Smoking Is A Health Hazard' becomes compulsory on cigarette packets in Australia

1974: Survey by ASH in Britain reveals that 86 per cent of tobacconists sell cigarettes to children

1975: Sir Richard Doll and Sir Richard Peto publish the results of a 20 years' study into the smoking habit of 35,000 doctors. It concludes that one in three smokers dies prematurely

1976: US Secretary of Health, Education and Welfare, Joseph Califano, calls cigarettes 'Public Health Enemy No 1' and says users are committing 'slow motion suicide'

1979: Marlboro sells 103.6 billion cigarettes, compared with Winston (81 billion) and Kool (56.7 billion)

1984: Nicotine gum introduced

1985: Californians for Non-Smokers' Rights relaunches as Americans for Non-Smokers' Rights

1988: First World No-Tobacco Day held by World Health Organization

1988: Joe Camel cartoon character created by British artist Nicholas Price for advertising campaigns introduced into America to celebrate 75th anniversary of Camel cigarettes

1992: Law to restrict the maximum tar content of a cigarette to 15mg introduced by the Council of Ministers in Brussels, signalling the demise of Senior Service, Capstan, and Gold Flake

1992: Nicotine patches introduced

1993: Environmental Protection Agency in US declares cigarette smoke to be a Class A carcinogen

1994: Tobacco taxes cut in Canada to eliminate smuggling

1994: Billboard advertising of tobacco products made illegal in Australia under the Tobacco Control Act

1995: American Medical Association devotes an entire issue of its journal to the dangers of smoking and the tactics of the tobacco industry

1996: National Spit Tobacco Education Programme (STEP) launched at a Philadelphia baseball game

1997: RJ Reynolds replaces the cartoon Joe Camel with new campaign

2001: Former Beatle George Harrison dies of lung cancer

INDEX

MacKenzie, Sir Compton 45, 49
Macleod, Iain 90
Malawi 55, 140-1
Manning, Thomas 111
'Marlboro man' 35, 118
Marsee, Sean 30
Marvell, Holt 49
Marx, Groucho 53
Marx, Karl 53
Mason-MacFarlane, General Sir Noel 85
Master Settlement Agreement (MAS) 133, 134, 135
Maugham, Somerset 53
Maya 67
Mayhugh, Bill 124
McCabe, Rolah 134
McQueen, Steve 8
Medical Research Council (UK) 90, 91
Melton, Larry 119
Merimee, Prosper 54
Michaelovitch, Grand Duke Michael 56
Millburn, Alan 34
Milligan, Spike 101-2
Mitchell, Joni 7
Molière 72
Montague, Pansy 22
Moorehead, Alan 84-5
Morris, Philip (and company) 19, 32, 35, 59, 78, 122, 132, 133, 135, 136, 137, 159, 160, 161
Moss, Kate 8
Muller, Franz Hermann 80-1
Murad the Cruel 71

Napoleon III, Emperor 60
National Fire Protection Association (US) 149
National Institute for Clinical Excellence (NICE) (UK) 120, 121
National Medical Journal For Doctors (US) 32
Navratilova, Martina 94
Newhart, Bob 8-9
Nicot, Jean 159
Nicotine
- advertising and sponsorship 33-4, 35-6
- chemical composition 102, 114
- chewing tobacco 50-1
- cigarettes (varieties) 55-6
- cigars (varieties) 54
- comparisons with other drugs 28, 44, 63
- costs of smoking 147-9
- cultivation/extraction process 138-42, 143-4
- first links with cancer 89-96
- health 25
- hookah 51-2
- 'lite' cigarettes 59
- litigation against manufacturers 133-4
- nature of addiction 43-6
- origin of name 69
- passive smoking 104-10
- physical effects 102-7, 111
- pipe industry 46, 47-9
- pregnancy and fertility 103, 105-7, 111
- qualities 12
- quitting smoking 111-24, 126, 127-8, 161
- reducing levels in the body 110-11
- role affected by World War I and II 82-7, 89
- sensory benefits 44
- smoking and stardom 37-40, 87-8
- snuff 49-50
- underage smoking 17-18
- worldwide cigarette manufacture 144-5

Niven, David 7
No Smoking/No Tobacco Days 27-8, 113, 161
Norway 144
Now, Voyage (movie) 87-8
Nurse, Sir Paul 121

O'Neill, Jonjo 31
Ogden, Chris 132, 143, 150-1
The Oxford Compact English Dictionary 45
Oxnam, Jane19

Parker, Sarah Jessica 8
Parker-Bowles, Camilla 111
Pepys, Samuel 12
Pershing, General John 83
Peru 69
Peter the Great 73
Peto, Sir Richard 90, 161
Philip III, King of Spain 73
Pocahontas 73, 159
Pope, Gina 32
The Pornographer (movie) 40
Portugal 68, 70
Presley, Elvis 99
Punch magazine (Australia) 22

Quayle, Anthony 85
Quit 113

Rains, Claude 88
Raleigh, Sir Walter 8, 9, 67, 70-1, 73, 159
Reader's Digest magazine 92
Reemtsma 137
Reitz, Gillian 31
Reynolds, Patrick 30-1
Reynolds, RJ (and company) 30, 132, 135, 137, 160, 161
Richmond, Surgeon General Julius 59
Roach, Hal 104
Rodgers, Anne-Toni 121
Rolfe, John 73, 74, 75, 138
Roman Catholicism 50
Roosevelt, Eleanor 53
Roosevelt, President Franklin D 7
Rothman, Louis 137, 160
Royal Canadian Legion 62
Royal College of Physicians 9, 18, 21-2, 25, 27, 45-6, 54, 64, 90, 91, 112, 118, 119, 125, 148, 153, 160
Royal London School of Medicine 105
Royal Society 12
Russell, Dr JS 23